Art and Life of Grandma Moses

MRS. ANNA MARY MOSES

EAGLE BRIDGE, NEW YORK

I anna mary Robertson, was born back in the green meadows and wild woods; on a Farm in washington, co. In the year of 1860, Sept 7. of Scotch Irish Paternal ancestry.

Here I spent the first ten years of my life with mother Father and Sisters and Brothers, those were my Happy days, free from care or worry, helping mother, rocking Sisters creadle. taking sewing lessons from mother sporting with my Brothers. making rafts to float over the mill pond, Roam the wild woods gathering Flowers, and building air castles,

The first page of Grandma Moses' Autobiography, written in 1945

Art and Life of GRANDMA MOSES

EDITED BY OTTO KALLIR

New York
The Gallery of Modern Art
1969

South Brunswick and New York: A. S. Barnes and Company
London: Thomas Yoseloff Ltd

A. S. Barnes and Company, Inc.
Cranbury, N. J. 08512

Thomas Yoseloff Ltd
108 New Bond Street
London W. 1, England

SBN: 498-07437-4

Printed in the United States of America

Contents

Grateful acknowledgment is expressed to those who have helped to make this exhibition possible through their generous loans and cooperation.

The Bennington Museum, Bennington, Vermont
The Phillips Collection, Washington, D.C.
The Phoenix Art Museum, Phoenix, Arizona
Memorial Art Gallery of the University of Rochester, New York
Webb Gallery of American Art, Shelburne Museum, Shelburne, Vermont
The Abby Aldrich Rockefeller Folk Art Collection, Williamsburg, Virginia
Mr. Irving Berlin, New York
Mr. and Mrs. Rudolf Bing, New York
Hallmark Cards, Incorporated, Kansas City
Mr. Victor Hammer, New York
Mr. and Mrs. Henry S. McNeil, Ft. Washington, Pennsylvania
Mrs. Hugh W. Moses, Hoosick Falls, New York
Mr. and Mrs. John M. Schiff, New York
and the anonymous lenders

LOUIS BROMFIELD

The well-known writer became acquainted with Grandma Moses at a very early date. The following essay was published as an introduction to *Grandma Moses: American Primitive* by Otto Kallir. Dryden Press, New York, 1946. Doubleday, Garden City, 1947.

ABOUT SIX OR SEVEN YEARS AGO I began hearing from friends living near Williamstown, Massachusetts, stories about a wonderful old woman who lived on a farm and painted pictures which she sold along with the jams and preserves she "put up" during the summer. She was, they said, prouder of her preserves than of her pictures and when she was asked the prices of her paintings she countered with a question "What size do you want?" The price depended on the size.

I would have suspected that the pictures were like the mediocrities exhibited at the average Middle Western County Fairs but for one fact: my friends said the pictures were remarkable and I respected their opinions because they had the background, the culture, the taste, and the understanding to know a real picture, a good picture, from a mediocrity or an affectation. They were not impressed by any artistic snobbery concerning "primitives" nor were they people to be entrapped by any nostalgic feeling for quaintness and the "good old days." They were buying Grandma Moses' pictures and had ordered some in advance, priced at her insistence, according to size.

And then I saw my first "Grandma Moses" and I understood their enthusiasm. What struck me immediately about the picture, and indeed about all the other "early Grandma Moses" which I saw, was the decorative quality and a kind of design and composition that I found in the Persian and Moslem Indian paintings I had seen in the East. In the pictures of Grandma Moses there was less formality, less smoothness, less minute attention to details but there was in both the New England and the Indian pictures the same sense of space and "of the whole" and above all a sense of the painter's intimate feeling for children and animals and color and the delights which only those can know who share intimate feeling for nature and have found for themselves a satisfactory relationship with the universe. As in the Indian pictures, each figure, animal or human, painted by Grandma Moses, was caught in an arrested moment of action . . . children skating, dogs running and barking, horses galloping and rearing. Clearly these were the pictures of someone who had loved and been loved and had borne children and lived close to animals and had had a busy, happy life. I knew without ever seeing her, that Grandma Moses was a wise, shrewd, happy old lady and that she painted for her own pleasure because she loved life and color and felt the necessity of communication to others through the medium, first of all of color, her own sense of the richness of life. It was clear that never in all her life had she known a bored moment . . . Her small world, whether viewed from her bedroom window, or from the window of a bus driving along the road, was at once a cosy and limitless universe which contained the keys to the knowledge of good living and understanding.

In those earlier pictures she often painted crudely, but this defect could not stifle the overwhelming sense of her satisfaction in life and her adjustment to the immense scheme of creation itself.

It is one of the remarkable things about Grandma Moses that after beginning to paint seriously late in life, she has gone on steadily learning and improving.

In the beginning she had to find her own way. She had to learn the kind of composition which gave her pleasure and satisfaction. She had to learn how to achieve the effects of color which so delighted her. She had even to learn about the materials and the tools she used and which ones permitted her to realize to the greatest degree the feeling she had inside her. She learned that a base of lustrous white, carefully prepared by her own methods after much experimentation, gave her pictures luminosity and even brilliance. She had to learn painfully and slowly how to achieve the hazy, constantly changing beauty of the distant Vermont hills and skies which she conveys so skillfully in her pictures. In fact she had to learn, herself, without help or advice, how to become a painter. As a result she always paints like herself.

I confess that for me many of Grandma Moses' pictures have a philosophical and at times even a literary appeal. She knows what country life feels like, and she conveys to the beholder the joy that is in a running colt, the singing beauty of a blossoming peach tree, the soothing peace of a clear, running brook. She does not paint any of these things separately, for themselves, but in a pattern, each in its proper relation to all the others. It is a pattern filled with the satisfaction of those who understand that any farm is a small but complete fragment of the universe in which all the laws of Nature are constantly in play, affecting the lives, the philosophy, and the faith of those who inhabit it.

There have been and are today many technically skillful artists who paint farm scenes and rural landscapes, but nearly all of them simply paint "pictures" adroit and sophisticated perhaps in design and color but without that luminosity, enthusiasm, and understanding which one finds in Grandma Moses' pictures. Too many of them are flat in spirit, with the smell of the studio about them. They reveal little inwardness or real warmth. They are simply pictorial, revealing or interpreting little or nothing.

A good farmer looking at most of the farm pictures and landscapes painted in our time might say "a pretty picture" or "no farm ever looked like that" and move on to the next one. In front of a Grandma Moses he would stop and chuckle and smile and sigh, for in it he would find not only every detail with satisfaction and understanding, but he would know at once that Grandma Moses understood his whole small world with its glories and hard work and those quick, deep inarticulate gusts of emotion which sweep over him at the sight of a newly born calf or a blossoming pear tree or at the smell of deep, rich soil, freshly turned to the warm sun in spring. He would recognize that Grandma Moses understood these fundamental things which make the good husbandman a part of the earth and the fullness thereof and make him invulnerable to the petty miseries and misfortunes which complicate and torment the lives of city-dwellers.

The great and increasing popularity of Grandma Moses with the general public and the increasing interest and appreciation of her pictures by more critical groups has its roots in the satisfaction of a special hunger which is steadily growing among all people in this Age of Aridity and Agitation. It is a hunger for something deeper, more spiritual, and more satisfactory than the materialist philosophies and political doctrines or even the art and writing born of the Industrial Revolution. In a world in which mechanical inventions and mass production have led man to worship the machine while it destroys his own higher capacities and makes a slave of him, the pictures of Grandma Moses give one a sense of the profound and fundamental goodness of small things, of the peace and confidence and satisfaction that comes of the adjusted and happy relationship of an individual to the whole of life, the universe and Eternity. The pictures of Grandma Moses are as far removed from the clash and monotony of a Detroit automobile factory as they are from the assembly line abstractions of the later Picasso or the decadent painting of the Sur-realists, both born of an industrial-mechanical age, one in approval of, one in revolt against, the materialism of a world which threatens to destroy itself or be destroyed by its very worship of automobiles and plumbing, of aeroplanes and atomic bombs.

In such a world the paintings of Grandma Moses provide a sense of peace and adjustment to the natural laws by which we must live or be destroyed. In Grandma Moses' world there is the same zest and understanding of the eternal importance of small things which one finds in the peasant pictures of Pieter Breughel. His pictures have the robustness and earthiness of a Flemish male.

Those of Grandma Moses are infused with the quality of a New England woman who had divided her life between two of the most beautiful parts of the world—the Shenandoah Valley and the hills of Vermont. But both Breughel and Grandma Moses tell you essentially the same thing—that every day life is good and amusing and filled with richness and variety and beauty, if you choose to find it.

At least that is what I find in a Grandma Moses picture, and I have seen the same satisfaction in the eyes of others standing before one of her paintings, studying the figures of a strutting Tom Turkey, or a rearing colt, or a blossoming tree, or a child skating on the ice of the clear little river she loves so well and paints so often.

JEAN CASSOU

One of the foremost European authorities on modern art and until recently director of the Musée National d'Art Moderne in Paris, wrote the following statement about Grandma Moses on the occasion of the artist's hundredth birthday in 1960.

Les naifs sont le sel de la terre. Grace à eux l'art de notre temps, le plus savant, le plus raffiné, le plus audacieux, conserve, en son fond, des sources de fraîcheur et de vie. Ainsi les Cubistes avaient-ils auprès d'eux le Douanier Rousseau, et leurs merveilleuses spéculations intellectuelles étaient garanties par le compagnonnage de ce cœur candide, animé en génie du peuple et de la nature. Les Etats-Unis sont aujourd'hui à l'avant-garde des plus hardies recherches esthétiques: mais ils ont aussi leurs forces originelles, leurs eaux vives. L'adorable Grandma Moses, dans con coin provincial, dans sa campagne, défend l'empire des feuillages et des oiseaux, maintient les droits de la nature. Elle nous donne à entendre qu'il y a encore un peu de paradis en ce monde et que l'art peut pousser ses pointes d'avant-garde aussi loin qu'il voudra parce qu'il a des racines profondément enfoncées en ce bon terreau du jardin de Grandma Moses.

The Primitives are the salt of the earth. Through their existence alone does contemporary art, so knowing, so sophisticated and daring, preserve in its depth sources of freshness and life. Thus the Cubists had at their side the Douanier Rousseau, and their marvelous intellectual speculations were counter-balanced by the companionship of this pure heart, inspired by the genius of the people and of nature. The United States through its "avant-garde" is making the most daring esthetic experiments, but also has its primeval forces, its springs of fresh water. From her small-town vantage point the adorable Grandma Moses comes to the defense of the countryside, the empire of foliage and birds, and upholds the rights of nature. She would have us know that there is still a bit of paradise left on this earth and that art may reach out as far as it will with its most advanced branches, because it is deeply rooted in the rich soil of Grandma Moses' garden.

JOHN CANADAY

The art critic of *The New York Times* is the author of the following essay, which was first published in "A Portfolio of Eight Paintings by Grandma Moses." *Art in America,* 1967.

Grandma Moses was too good to be true, but true she was, in senses of the word that keep expanding as you think about her. Her phenomenal popularity came in very large part from the public's feeling that in an age of disillusion here was something that could be clung to as truth. At the time when Grandma Moses appeared, the public that was waiting for her had had just enough education in art theory to know that there was something called "primitive" art that was supposed to come spontaneously from the heart, from an instinctively directed talent or rare exception among amateur dabblers, something that could be trusted as genuine art because the theorists said it was, but something that could be understood directly, without bothersome estheticizing, simply on the basis of its surface allure.

However misguided these ideas may have been, Grandma Moses more than filled the bill for their popular application. In 1939, when she made her debut with three paintings at the Museum of Modern Art (an additional assurance that it was safe to admit you liked her), the middle-aged portion of this country's population was reeling from the shock of a depression that had knocked into smithereens a dream that had survived even the shock of World War I—the dream of a halcyon America invulnerable to the ills that had sickened Europe for centuries (although good old degenerate Europe had managed, somehow, to survive), a dream that had been inculcated by several generations of idealistic schoolteachers, by the verses of James Whitcomb Riley and by mistaken interpretations of what the world of Huckleberry Finn and Tom Sawyer was all about.

The nostalgia for an American past that seemed idyllic had inspired Eugene O'Neill to write *Ah, Wilderness!* and had made a success of that play when it was produced in 1932. Grandma Moses went even further back into our past and assured us that it was still there and a part of our heritage, just as it had truly been a part of her life. Born in 1860, she began—in her late 70s—to recall her childhood and girlhood in images that were all the more convincing for taking on (as true "primitive" painting always does) an air of dream. Genre painters of the latter half of the 19th century who recorded on the spot the snows, the summers, the festivities, the labors and the domestic routines that Grandma Moses recorded from loving memory, are not half as convincing as she is, and not a tenth, or a twentieth, or a hundredth, as affecting.

She had in addition a personal quality that the public expects of an artist but is not often given—her identity, as a human being, with the spirit projected by her art. She could not have been more perfect for her role. She had the kind of beauty that in a woman's old age can stir the observer to speculations upon her entrancing aspect in youth, but is devoid of the decayed sexuality that makes the old age of some once-beautiful women tragic. The configurations of her bony face became more beautiful each year as she approached the magical, the incredible birthday of a hundred years. And she never failed, not once, not in any statement, or posed photograph, or for that matter in a painting—whether the painting was one of her best or one of her many minor efforts—to live up to the legend.

She was expertly managed—and this came to be held against her, as if an artist should not profit from her work. (Ask Giotto about that; ask Titian; ask Rubens; ask Picasso.) "Grandma Moses isn't a person," we began to say, "she's an industry." But she was not a part of the extension of her art into the commercial channels that made her name a byword. She painted, and other people took care of the rest. She continued to paint for the same reason that she began to paint, as a form of autobiographical pleasure that would have given her the same joy even if she had never had the additional and unexpected pleasure of fame.

Was she really a good painter?—or, to use a word less popular today, was she really a good artist? She was. She was acutely observant not only of the details of landscape (and how broad, how deep, her landscapes can be, for all the intimacy of their detail) but of the interrelationships of hills and valleys, of streams or rivers and the levels that determine their courses, of houses and barns and churches as outgrowths of landscape in spots properly chosen for them by people who unquestioningly regarded their life and its practical adjuncts as an integration with the terrain. In the distance of the picture called "In Harvest Time" there is a rounded hill covered partly with cultivated fields, partly with woods. In most "primitive" painting and perhaps even more in the work of sophisticated painters these areas would have been reduced to an arbitrary patchwork. But in "In Harvest Time" each division lies upon its segment of the total contour with an inevitable rightness—a minor passage of the kind that makes the world of Grandma Moses so convincing.

She had, too, a wonderful skill in the disposition of figures in landscape that made them its true and natural inhabitants. No figure is casual or incidental. In the technical-academic sense, Grandma Moses could not draw, but in the purest sense she was an expressive draftsman who could, for example, describe each of the busy people in "A Frosty Day" with such economy and truth that there is no more question as to their rightness in their sweet little world than there is as to the rightness of Bruegel's figures in his snowy cosmos. Is it necessary to admit that this artist who painted more than 1600 pictures was not at her best on all occasions? (Was Giotto? Was Titian? Was Rubens? Is Picasso?) Is it necessary to point out that if she is not in the company of the masters, neither are they in hers? These circumstances are beside the main point, which is that Grandma Moses was a true artist—too good to be true, but true all the same, and truer and truer the more you think about her.

ON THE ART AND LIFE OF GRANDMA MOSES

By OTTO KALLIR

Grandma Moses is called a "primitive." Her paintings show plainly that their author has had no art training. She tried to make her pictures look as natural as possible and sometimes went so far as to use "glitter" on her winter landscapes in order to make the snow appear more realistic. To a friend who tried to dissuade her from this practice, she once said: "Have you never been in the country on a sunny winter's day? You would have seen how the sun shines on the snow and makes it sparkle all over." In spite of such naturalistic endeavors, details are often drawn "wrong" or are clumsily represented. And yet every picture painted by Grandma Moses emanates harmony, sincerity and purity of purpose to such a high degree that you forget its shortcomings. The simplicity of her rendering, the childlike way in which she seems to ignore technical difficulties, are so convincing that her pictures cast a spell over the beholder. Her works have now found general recognition. The great public loves them—but so do circles that are wont to be sharply critical in their art appreciation. The longing for a simplicity that we have lost—not in the field of art alone—the yearning for peace, for contact with nature, which is growing more and more remote, perhaps the nostalgia for a childhood in which everything seemed simple and uncomplicated—all this draws us towards the paintings of Grandma Moses.

Grandma Moses is called a "primitive"—but what is a "primitive painter?" It is important not to confuse "primitive" with "self-taught." During recent years it has become customary to label as primitive almost everything originating from the hand of self-

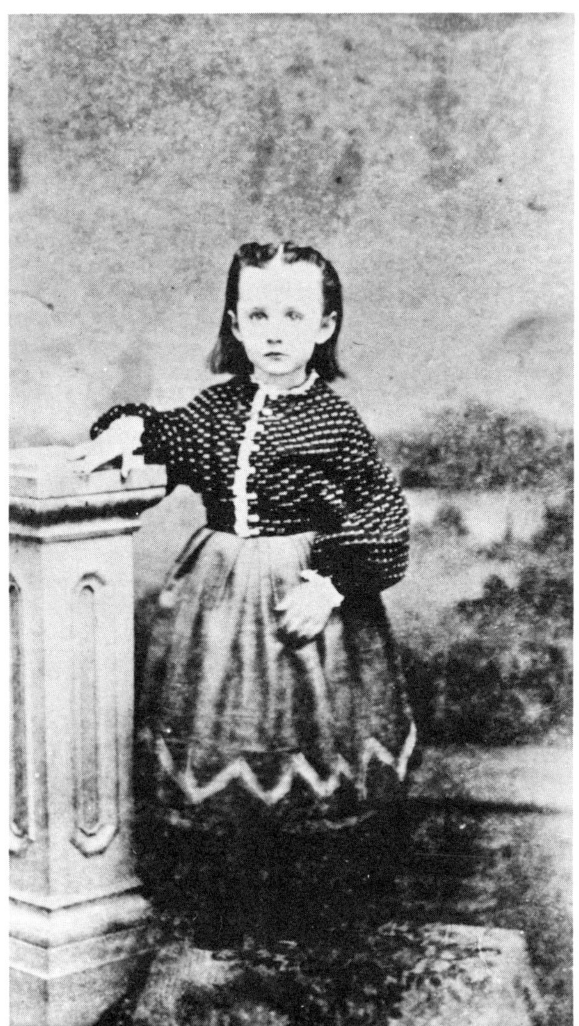

Anna Mary Robertson, 4 years old

taught painters; to those who use the word in this inclusive fashion, style does not seem important. Such a superficial view of the subject has had a simplifying effect, for it has created an extremely large group of so-called "primitives." Actually it has joined together in a single category two different conceptions.

Primitive painters are almost certain to be self-taught, but self-

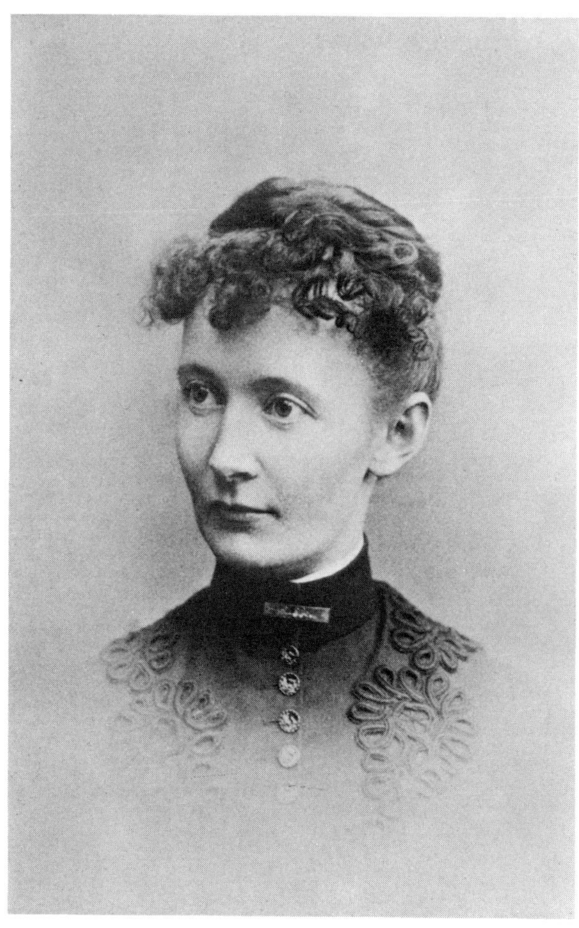

Anna Mary Robertson Moses as bride, 1887

taught painters may adopt any style to express themselves. They are not bound to any special form—to any limitation of idea and content, as are primitive artists. The style of a talented self-taught painter need not differ from that of a professional, whereas a primitive work is always distinct from that of a professional artist. This does not imply that primitive art is inferior, or, as we sometimes hear, a mere by-path of art. A good primitive picture has all the fundamental qualities of a good professional picture. If the creative motive that inspired a work was honest, if the artist can formulate his idea and recreate it in the beholder, his work is true art, whether produced with the help of schooling or not.

To a rare degree, the work of Grandma Moses lives up to what we expect in a primitive painting. She knew nothing about art training. The only artistic inspiration within her reach consisted of illustrated school books, Christmas cards, nineteenth century color prints, and illustrations in magazines. One cannot set a definite date for the beginning of her artistic production because, almost without being aware of it, she had done some painting on and off throughout her life.

Her first works relied strongly on the examples of art which she had seen in illustrated books: she began to copy them. But even at this early stage she strove not to produce merely an imitation, but to transform it into something of her own. For example, in a copy of the famous Currier and Ives print "Home for Thanksgiving," the color and atmosphere she lends to the picture surpass the original. She has made something new out of it, has given her personal style to the old composition. And this style can be found in all her paintings. It is so striking that every one of them can be immediately recognized as her work.

Her pictures are typical of America, more especially of the countryside where the State of New York borders on Vermont. The Moses farm is situated in the Hoosick Valley, a lovely panorama of rolling hills through which the Hoosick River winds its way, with the Green Mountain Range silhouetted in the distance. This is the landscape she knew and loved for a lifetime and where, year in and year out, she watched the passing seasons.

Yet only a very few of her paintings were "done from nature."

The idea of sitting out in the open with all her painting equipment did not appeal to her. She considered it "very impractical." After coming indoors from a ride in the neighborhood, from a little trip to visit some relatives, or simply from looking across the valley from the steps of her porch, she would sit down at her table and start a picture to record the impressions she had just received.

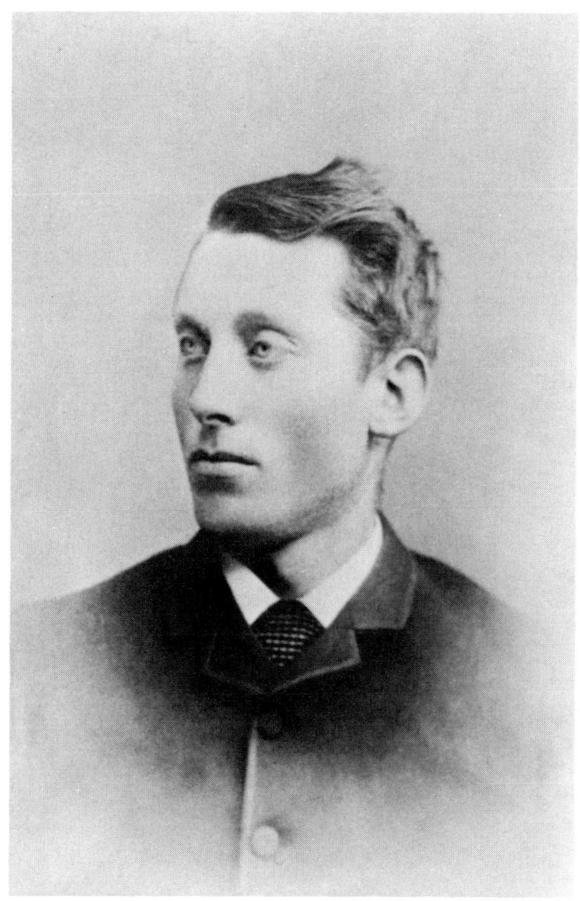

Thomas Salmon Moses as bridegroom, 1887

Sometimes she went far back in her memories, to her early married years, when she lived in Virginia. All these familiar scenes, dear to her and part of her very being, form the setting for various events that have taken place in more or less remote times: memories of her own childhood; stories she heard when she was young (and

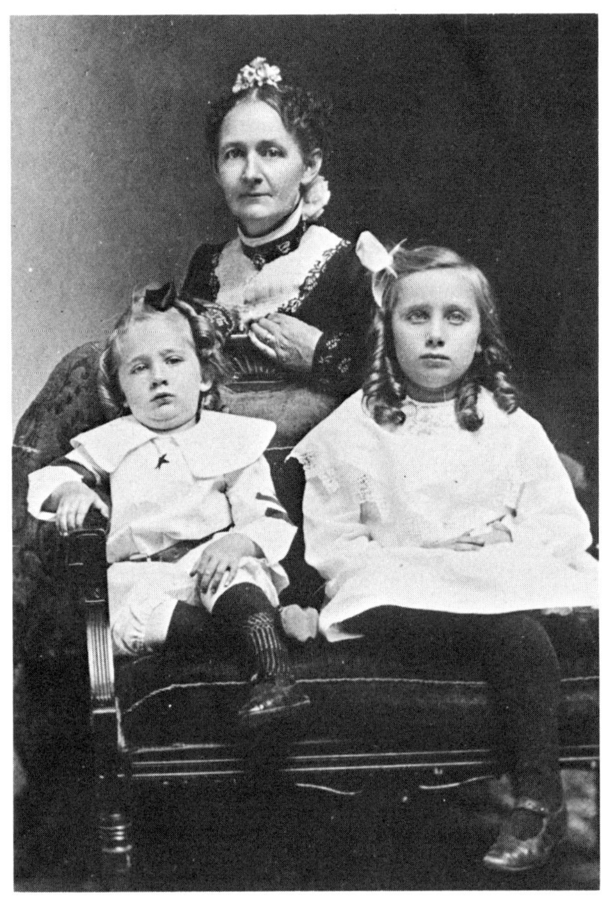

Grandma Moses with two of her children, Hugh and Anna, ca. 1903

which were old even then); anecdotes about her forefathers who lived in this same Hoosick Valley; history and folklore. She transmuted into painting songs she learned in her youth and which she still knew by heart, for instance, "The Old Oaken Bucket." She was careful not to omit a single detail: every person, flower, or tree mentioned in the song had to appear in her painting. Observing her at work, one was impressed by the way she lived with the picture she was working on. She would tell what events had taken place in the houses she was about to paint, and how the two farms in her picture were once linked by the story of a romantic love. Her work was not finished before all the persons and all the flowers of the song had been put into it. The pleasure Grandma Moses took in making a picture, the playful imagination which went into every little detail, can be felt in the completed work: it always remains fresh and fascinating, it never grows dull, no matter how often one looks at it.

While the range of Grandma Moses' artistic expression is limited, she mastered that range thoroughly. Whatever her subject may be—whether "Sugaring-Off," or "Washday," or "Country Fair," or just "Sunday"—one always feels that it is her Sunday and her washday. She never succeeded in producing a picture that went beyond her well known and familiar sphere; each of her pictures represents some small part of her own life. The world of her paintings is bright and serene. Everything always seems in perfect harmony; she did not consider disagreeable and troublesome subjects. She loved color and used it to give her pictures an abundance of life, freshness and radiance. She did not regard gloomy colors as the "right thing" for a painter.

Grandma Moses' first "works" were small yarn pictures, mostly landscapes, very skillfully executed in bright colors and copied from illustrations. The same subjects were repeated later in her paintings and it is interesting to note how quickly she adapted herself to the new technique of oil. But for the most part, these efforts are only of historical interest. Not until she undertook a subject that meant something to her from personal experience did she come into her own; one of her early "Sugaring-Off" pictures already shows the characteristics of the artist's style and can be counted among her best works.

Grandma Moses' first one-man show took place in New York at the Galerie St. Etienne. It was called "What A Farm Wife Painted" and opened on October 9, 1940. Public and press reacted with generous sympathy, although the exhibition included many of her early attempts in which her remarkable talent was scarcely visible.

THE GALERIE ST ETIENNE

REQUESTS THE HONOR OF YOUR COMPANY
AT THE PREVIEW OF THE EXHIBITION

WHAT A FARM WIFE PAINTED
WORKS BY MRS. ANNA MARY MOSES

BORN GREENWICH, N. Y., 1860

ON WEDNESDAY, OCTOBER 9TH 1940
FROM NINE TO ELEVEN O'CLOCK IN THE EVENING

46 WEST 57TH STREET NEW YORK CITY

Invitation to Grandma Moses' First One-Man Exhibition

During the years that followed, Grandma Moses painted a large number of pictures, and the progress she had made since her first appearance in the art world could be clearly recognized. There was no longer any doubt about her extraordinary talent. The style had grown more assured, the coloring more discreet. She now handled delicate hues with a mastery which her early works had seldom achieved. The outlines had grown softer, and she reached astonishing effects of depth. Some of the most striking pictures which originated during this period are reproduced in this book. "Black Horses," for instance, shows a light green, hilly landscape with mountains in the background. The different shades of green in the meadows and fields are wonderfully brought out. In order to give depth to the picture, she framed the landscape with trees on both sides, a group of birches to the left and a single tree to the right, like a stage setting. The trees grow out of a narrow strip of land in the foreground, which enhances the impression of looking into a wide green valley. The black horses are seen cantering around the tree on the right. As with some of her figures, the drawing is faulty and awkward, yet the horses focus one's attention so strongly upon

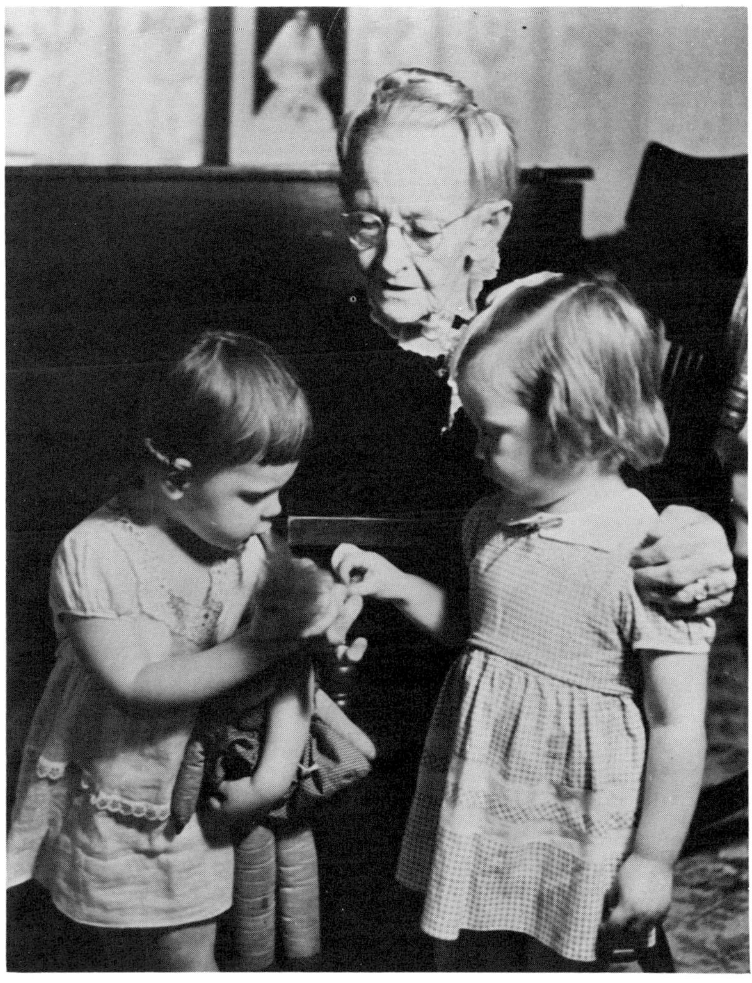

Grandma Moses with two of her Great-grandchildren, 1952

themselves that one takes them for the main object of the painting, and the landscape becomes merely a setting for them. One could almost call the composition of this picture sophisticated, if it did not, at the same time, impress one as utterly naive and simple.

The instinctive mastery of coloring and composition, shown perhaps for the first time in "Black Horses," comes to light in

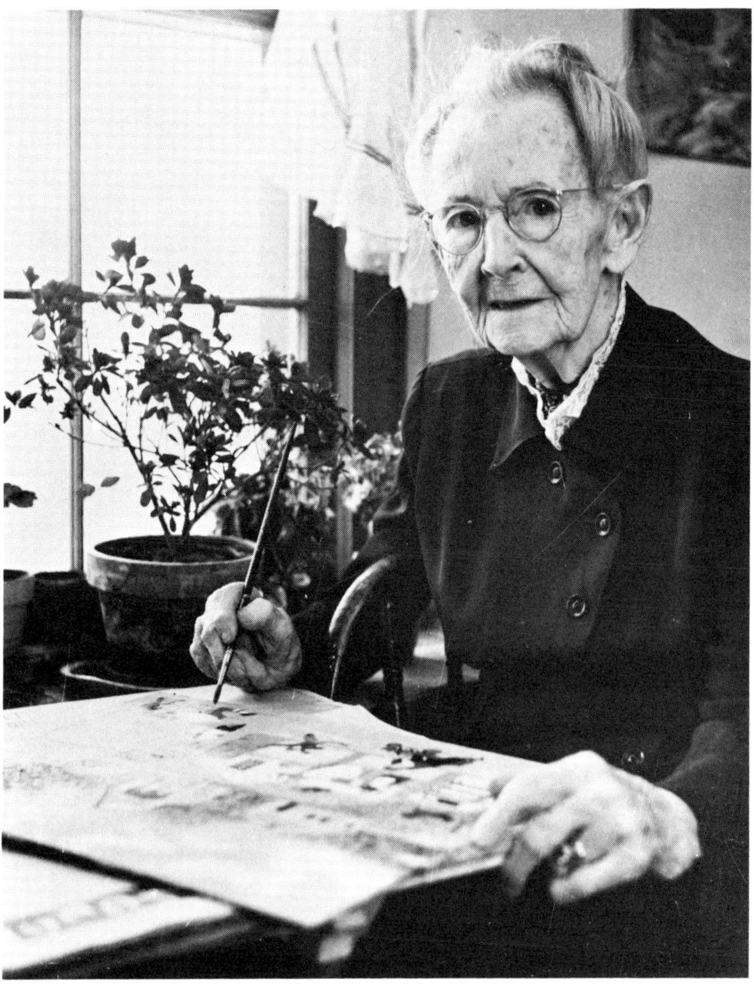

Grandma Moses Painting, 1955

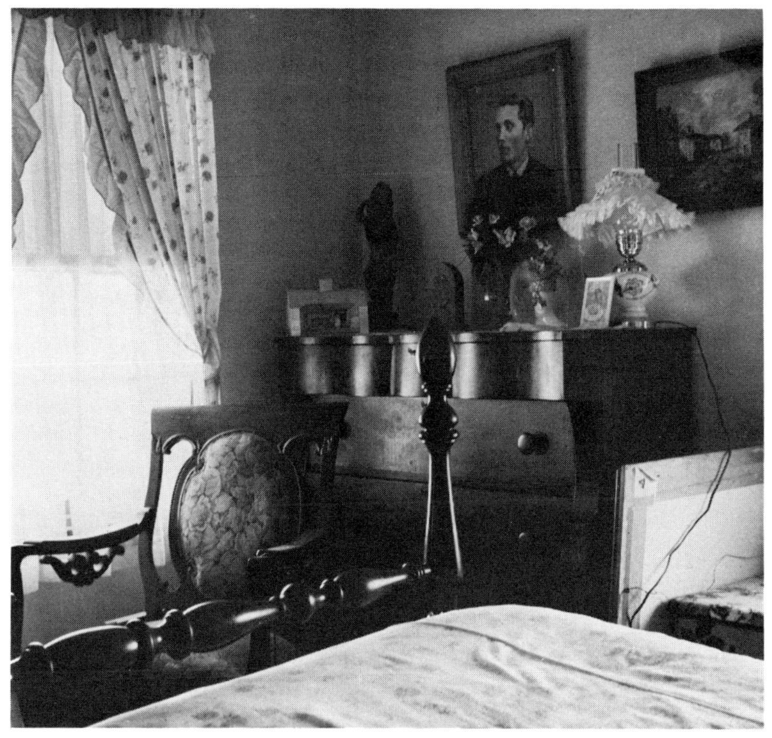

Bedroom of Grandma Moses

subsequent pictures. The works of this period are among her best and most popular. To name but a few: "The Old Oaken Bucket," "Over the River to Grandma's House," new versions of "Sugaring-Off" and "Catching the Turkey" themes; views of "Hoosick Falls"; and the "Checkered House," which brought her as an exhibitor to the Metropolitan Museum of Art in New York when that painting was one of a hundred and fifty selected from among five thousand, to form the "Portrait of America" show.

Soon Grandma Moses began to receive fan mail from all over the country. People who had seen reproductions of her works wrote to ask whether she would paint them again. Eager to please everybody, Grandma Moses accepted "orders" of this kind. She regarded all those who wanted her pictures as friends whom she could not and would not disappoint. Thus she sometimes found herself obliged to repeat her most successful paintings, although she did not enjoy it. However, they offer an interesting insight into her method of work. I once asked her how she was able to

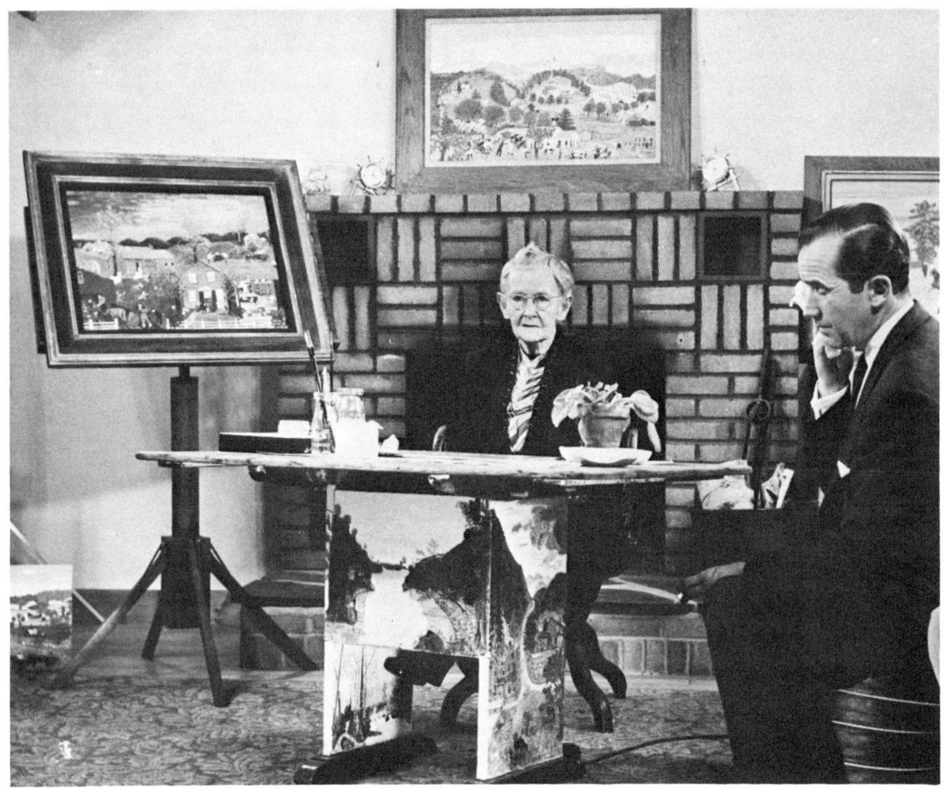

Grandma Moses is interviewed by Edward R. Murrow, 1955. She is seated at her Tip-Up Table. At left, the painting "Halloween," above "The Battle of Bennington."

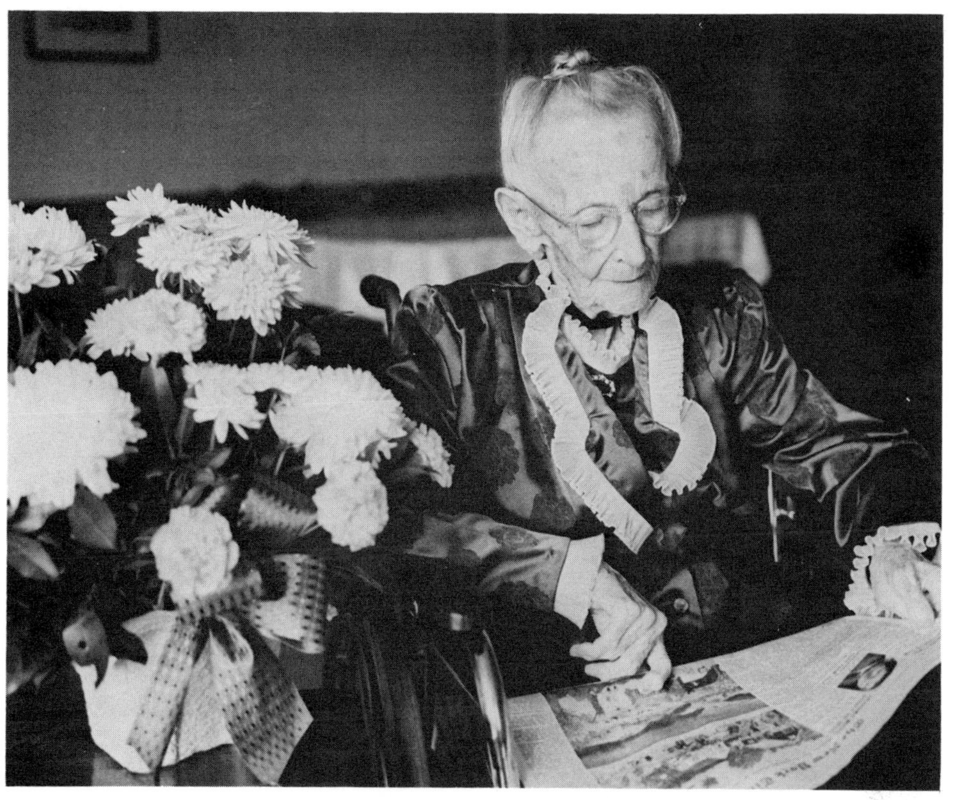

Grandma Moses on her 101st Birthday

avoid exact repetitions and to add new aspects to a given subject as, for instance, "The Checkered House," which she had painted several times. She explained that she imagined looking at a scene through a window, the window being the frame for the picture. When she wanted to paint another "Checkered House," she needed only to look out of this "window" at another angle, and then "The Checkered House" would move in her imagination from the left to the right side of the painting.

Almost all of Grandma Moses' paintings are done on strong masonite board. The size of her pictures rarely exceeds twenty-four by thirty inches. At first they were much smaller, but later she settled upon the size of about eighteen by twenty-four inches, which she liked best. She used canvas only at the very beginning, and for a small group of large pictures done between the years 1943 and

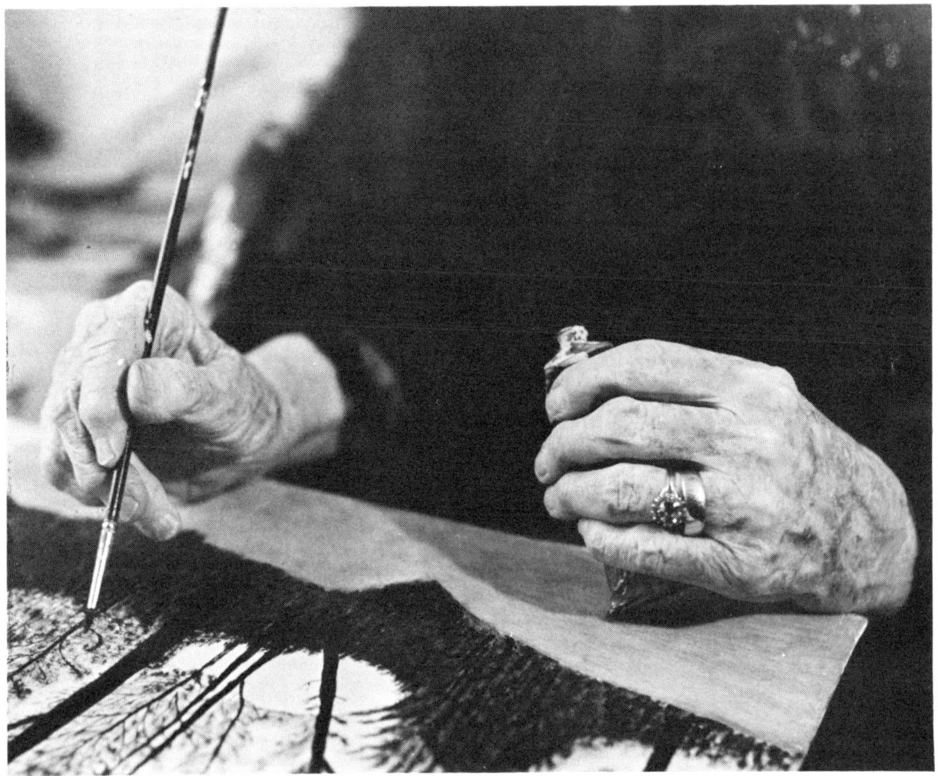

The Hands of Grandma Moses

1951. Having acquired a certain practice in the handling of spaces, she permitted herself in these large paintings an astonishing freedom of line and color.

It is hard to tell exactly how many pictures Grandma Moses painted. She worked long over some of them; others, especially variations of earlier subjects, were quickly completed. She treated new subjects more elaborately, of course, trying out her colors and often toning down a harsh red or blue to make it blend with the atmosphere of the picture.

Soon after her first exhibition, Grandma Moses' brother, Fred E. Robertson, felt she should keep a record of the paintings she sold. He gave her a notebook, bound in black boards, and had labels printed to be attached to the back of the paintings. The artist followed her brother's advice. She kept fairly accurate records in the book, and nearly all her paintings, completed after she received the labels, show the date, number and title.

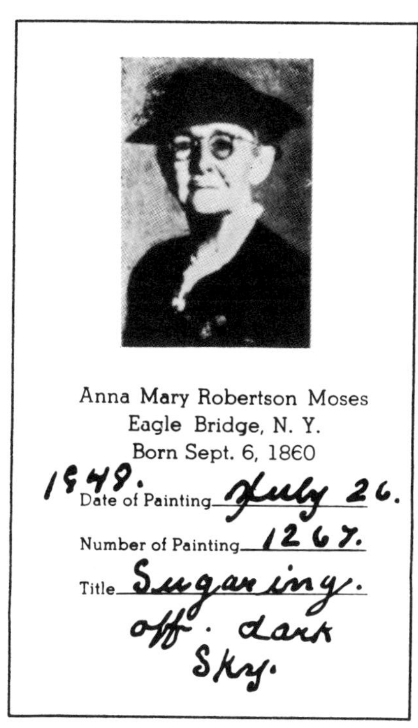
Anna Mary Robertson Moses
Eagle Bridge, N. Y.
Born Sept. 6, 1860

1949. Date of Painting July 26.

Number of Painting 1267.

Title Sugaring. off. dark Sky.

4

Painting Number	Year Completed	Title of painting
1942, Feb		a long Road, sold for $4.00 to mr callor, ny. city
" "		Tolles pasture " " " " " " "
" "		the Debate " " " " " " "
" "		the Covared Bridge in winter, sold to mr callor, For $2,00
" "		when the cows come Home, sold to mr callor, For $200
		porring wax, sold, For $20,00 mr Callor, ny, city
		Fishgard a welsh Farm, no 1 and 2,

Page from the artist's notebook

But in spite of this impressive "bookkeeping," the information given on the labels and in the book is not always correct. Some numbers occur twice, others are omitted altogether. The old lady now and then seemed to lose track of them. The dating too is sometimes inaccurate: many pictures bear the same date. This is to be explained by the fact that Grandma Moses had set herself cer-

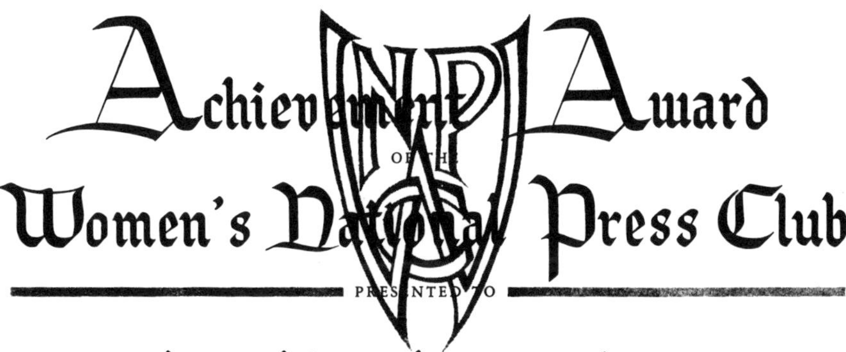

Achievement Award
of the
Women's National Press Club
presented to
Anna Mary Robertson Moses
FOR OUTSTANDING ACCOMPLISHMENT IN
Art

May 14, 1949

Dorothy E. Williams
PRESIDENT

Congratulations & continued success
Harry Truman

Achievement Award of the Women's National Press Club presented by President Truman, May 14, 1949

tain days of delivery on which she dispatched several pictures at the same time. An entire group of paintings, regardless of when they had actually been completed, thus received the same date. But it also happened that she dated certain pictures several months ahead.

An introduction to the art of Grandma Moses would be incomplete without a few words about her personality. Physically slight, she was a very active woman. Her intelligent personality made a strong impression on everyone who met her. She had most definite ideas and opinions of her own, went her own way, was not easily ruffled by anything. She showed much interest in the events of the day as well as in the people around her and remained lively and active into her old age. She had a wonderful sense of humor and would speak about the shortcomings of her fellow men with a twinkle in her eye, but never in a sarcastic way. Her kind and good-natured approach was felt in her personal presence as well as in her work. She enjoyed telling stories, mostly memories of when she was young, of the days she evoked in many of her pictures.

*

There is hardly a career in the history of modern painting comparable to that of Grandma Moses. Much has been written about her and her art, and she has become America's best known and best loved painter. The contrast between her life as a simple farm woman and her sudden fame in later years caught the imagination of a wide public here and abroad. Her "success story" has tended to put undue emphasis on the outward signs of recognition and to obscure her artistic achievement. Now that more than seven years have elapsed since Grandma Moses died in Hoosick Falls, N. Y., on December 13, 1961, at the age of 101, her work can be objectively evaluated. The present show has been arranged to serve this purpose.

From Writings by Grandma Moses

HOW I PAINT

When I first commenced to paint with oil, I thought every painting would be my last one, so I was not so interested. Then the requests commenced to come for this one and that one. "Paint me one just like that one!" so I have painted on and on, till now. I think I am doing better work than at first, but it is owing to better brushes and paint. The brushes help greatly, I can get now little brushes, I couldn't get at one time during the war, sometimes I had to use a match. And the colors now are good, and then I got so that I can mix them and do better work with them.

Before I start painting, I get a frame, then I saw my masonite board to fit the frame. (I always thought it a good idea to build the sty before getting the pig, likewise with young men, get the home before the wedding.)

Then I go over the board with linseed oil, then with three coats of flat white paint to cover up the darkness of the board. With two coats, the dark would strike through in some places, and three give it body, so when you start to paint the picture, you don't have to put on so much of the colored paint. The tube paint is quite expensive, and you have to use it accordingly, that's a Scotch idea, you see. Now the board is ready for the scene, whatever the mind may produce, a landscape, an old bridge, a dream, or a summer or winter scene, childhood memories, but always something pleasing

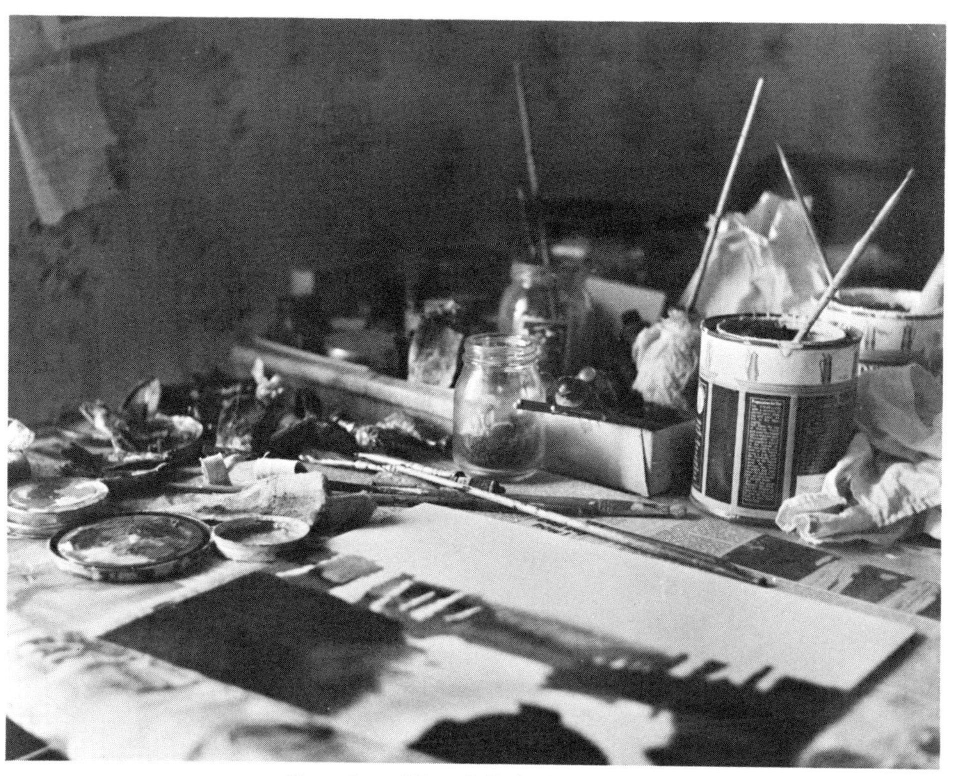
Grandma Moses' Painting Table

and cheerful, I like bright colors and activity. I use masonite or hard wood to paint on, because it will last many years longer than canvas. Sometimes the frames are hard to obtain, they may be pretty frames, but in dilapidated condition, then I must use hammer and nails and plastico. The frames should always blend with the paintings for best effect.

When I paint, I study and study the outside lots of times. Often I get at loss to know just what shade of green, and there are a hundred trees that have each three or four shades of green in them. I look at a tree and I see the limbs, and then the next part of the tree is a dark, dark black green, then I have got to make a little lighter green, and so on. And then on the outside, it'll either be a yellow green, or whitish green, that's the way the trees are shaded. And the snow—they tell me that I should shade it more or use more blue, but I have looked at the snow and looked at the snow and looked at the snow, and I can see no blue, sometimes there is a little shadow, like the shadow of a tree, but that would be grey instead of blue, as I see it. I love pink, and the pink skies are beautiful. Even as a child, the redder I got my skies with my father's old paint, the prettier they were.

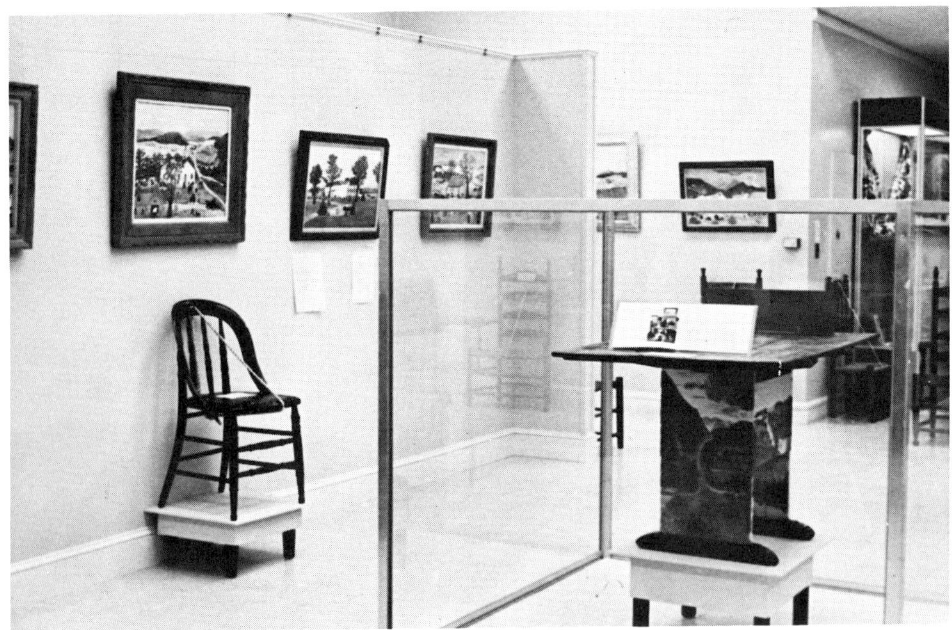

Tip-Up Table. Grandma Moses Gallery, Bennington Museum

MY TIP-UP TABLE

I have an old tip-up table, that my aunt gave me 35 years ago, it was built for a log cabin.

Back in the 18th century, Phinious Whiteside came and made his home in the township of Washington Co., N. Y., taking up a large track of land on which he made his home.

He had a large family of girls and boys; when his oldest son became of age he gave him his portion, which was the custom in those days, a freedom suit, so many sheep, an ax and I think 200 acres of land, and said, now go and build a home for your self.

He went into the 200 acres of heavy timber which joined his father's, cut down trees and built himself a one room log cabin, then he built himself a bed, and a trundle-bed, then the tipback table, so as when the trundle-bed was run out, there would be room enough to move about. The table was made of pine planks. Under the top between the standards there was a box in which they kept their pewter dishes, this had a plank cover so that it formed a chair.

Long years after the new large brick house was built, the table was moved over into the cellar and used as a milk table for many more years. Then one day my aunt sent it to me for a flower stand; I have painted scenes on the standards and covered the top with postal cards, and now use it for my easel on which I paint.

WORK AND HAPPINESS

Now that I am 95 years old, looking back over the years, I have seen many changes take place, so many inventions have been made, things now go faster, in olden times things were not so rushed. I think people were more content, more satisfied with life than they are today, you don't hear nearly as much laughter and shouting as you did in my day, and what was fun for us wouldn't be fun now. They used to get together, a certain bunch, and they would ride down the hill on sleighs or scoop shovels. It was harmless fun and not dangerous. Another thing we used to do in the winter was go on hayrides. It would be announced at the school that they would meet at such a place. They would get somebody's horses to haul them, so you know they didn't go very swift. They would put the hay rack or body of a wagon on top of a bob sleigh, they would pile loose hay on the rack, and then all got on to that, wrapped warm for the ride. They would have their music as they went along, some of them would play on jew's-harps, some of them would have horns, and then with their yelling and laughing, it made a pretty noisy load. They would go maybe ten or twelve miles and back again. They would do it in the evenings, they had to get home anyway by 12 o'clock. Nowadays there is no snow on the roads, and they go to the drive-in movies. I think laughter has a great deal to do with one's feelings, and a good hearty laughter gives you an animated feeling that carries you on again.

In this age I don't think people are as happy, they don't take time to be happy, they are worried. They are too anxious to get ahead of their neighbor, they are striving and striving to get something better. I do think in a way they have too much now.

We did with much less. My grandfather came into this country and learned the shoemaker's trade, and my mother was twelve years old before she had a pair of boughten shoes. Where he'd work, they would give him the tops of old shoes, and out of those he'd make the shoes for the children.

Any child who had twelve cents, why, he was rich; and think of it now, they'd throw it to the winds, they don't stop to count pennies. It was chiefly barter in those days, they would exchange their eggs and butter and all their grain for whatever they wanted from the store. If two people wanted to get married, and they were young they would go on horseback to the minister, they would take along a sack of beans or something to that effect to pay the minister, because the minister had to have food. Now money is master.

Within the last fifty years it is much easier to make a living. My sons work shorter hours than we did. My husband used to get up and milk thirty cows in the morning, now no man would think they could do such a thing, they depend on machinery to do all the milking, it's labor saving. But people have not changed, they are only keeping pace with the present age.

Work of any description adds to one's happiness, no matter what it is. If anybody is occupied all the time, and they keep their mind in their work, they have no time to think of their worries, and I believe, with children, the sooner you can teach them to commence to do things, the happier they are, the prouder they are. When I was a child, I would always help Mother with different things in the house. She might be cutting out some material and she might say: "Anna Mary, you can have all those giblets for your dolls' clothes." How I would work for it, to get all those pieces. Maybe the work that she would want me to do would be to fill the wood box, or fill the reservoir in back of the stove, it would hold six pails of water, we had to bring the water upstairs from the well in the cellar; to bring it up was quite a chore.

I have kept busy all my life. It seems foolish to sleep when there is so much to do all over. There is always something to do and to work for, you must never give up. . . .

*

Grandma Moses concluded her autobiography, My Life's History, *with the following words:*

I look back on my life like a good day's work, it was done and I feel satisfied with it. I was happy and contented, I knew nothing better and made the best out of what life offered. And life is what we make it, always has been, always will be.

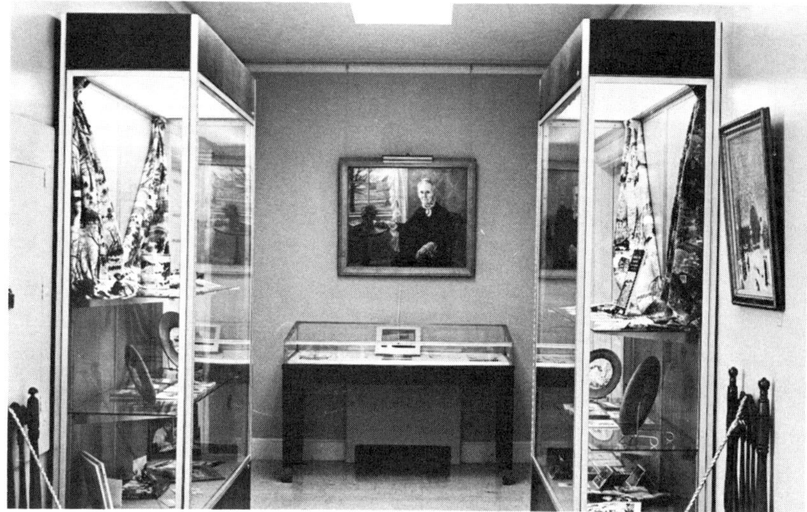

Room in the Grandma Moses Gallery, The Bennington Museum

BIOGRAPHICAL DATA

1860	September 7. Anna Mary Robertson born in Greenwich, N. Y.
From 1872	Working as a hired girl on neighboring farms.
1887	Married Thomas Salmon Moses.
1887–1905	Living in Virginia. Ten children born; five died in infancy.
1905	Returned to New York State; bought farm in Eagle Bridge, N. Y.
ca. 1920	First picture painted on the fireboard in the parlor; and landscapes decorating the panels of the "tip-up table."
1927	Thomas Salmon Moses dies.
1930's	Beginning to paint in earnest. Exhibiting pictures along with her preserves at county fairs.
1939	Exhibits pictures in window of drugstore in Hoosick Falls, where Louis J. Caldor discovers them. Three paintings in show of "Contemporary Unknown American Painters" in the Members' Room of the Museum of Modern Art, New York.

1940 First one-man show, entitled "What a Farm Wife Painted," at the Galerie St. Etienne, New York.

1941 New York State Prize presented to Grandma Moses for "The Old Oaken Bucket" at the Syracuse Museum of Fine Arts.

1941–to date Hundreds of one-man and group exhibitions in the United States.

1946 Publication of *Grandma Moses: American Primitive,* by Otto Kallir, with introduction by Louis Bromfield and autobiographical notes by Grandma Moses.

1947 Award of Distinctive Merit, Art Directors Club, New York.

1949 Women's National Press Club Award "for outstanding accomplishment in art," presented to Grandma Moses by President Harry S. Truman in Washington, D. C.

1949 Honorary Doctorate, Russell Sage College, Troy, New York.

1949 Documentary color film, narrated by Archibald MacLeish.

1950 Six one-man shows in Europe (Vienna, Munich, Salzburg, Berne, The Hague, Paris).

1951 Honorary Doctorate, Moore Institute of Art, Philadelphia, Pa.

1952 Publication of *My Life's History,* by Grandma Moses.

1953 Guest of the New York Herald Tribune Forum.

1955–56 Nine one-man shows in Europe (Bremen, Stuttgart, Cologne, Hamburg, Oslo, London, Aberdeen, Edinburgh, Glasgow).

1960–61 Proclamation by Governor Nelson A. Rockefeller, declaring the artist's birthday as "Grandma Moses Day" in the State of New York.

1961 December 13. Death of Grandma Moses at the Health Center, Hoosick Falls, N. Y.

1960–64 Exhibition entitled "My Life's History," first shown in New York at the I.B.M. Gallery, then presented under the sponsorship of the Smithsonian Institution at museums in nine American cities, thereafter at museums in European countries: Austria, France, Germany, Norway, Finland, Sweden, Denmark, and at the Pushkin Museum in Moscow.

1968 Opening of the Grandma Moses Gallery at The Bennington Museum, Vermont.

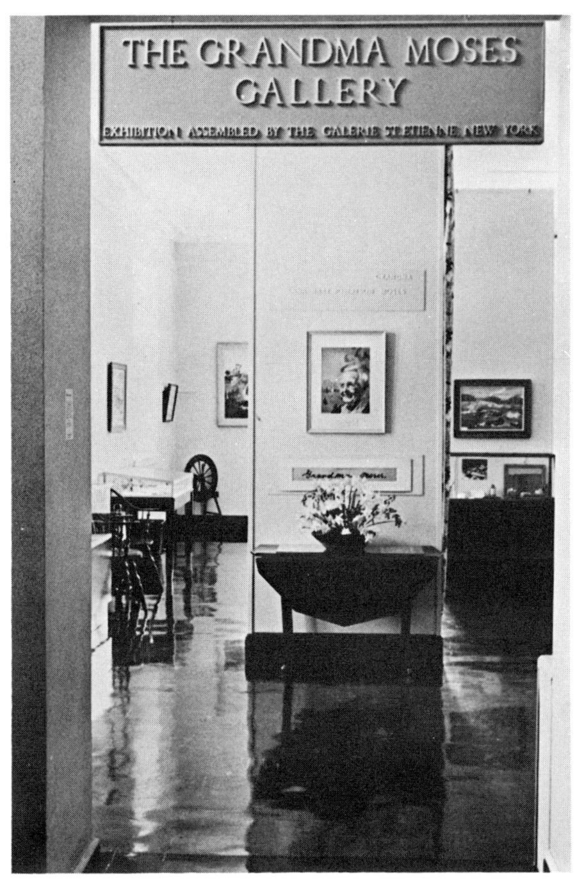

Paintings by Grandma Moses are in many museums and private collections in this country and abroad, among them:

The White House, Washington, D. C.
The Metropolitan Museum of Art, New York
Minneapolis Institute of Arts, Minneapolis, Minn.
William Rockhill Nelson Gallery, Kansas City, Mo.
Pasadena Art Museum, California
Rochester Memorial Gallery, Rochester, New York
Museum of Art, Rhode Island School of Design, Providence, Rhode Island
Syracuse Museum of Fine Arts, New York
The Phillips Gallery, Washington, D. C.
Birmingham Museum of Art, Alabama
Parrish Art Museum, Southampton, New York
Phoenix Art Museum, Arizona
Art Museum, University of California, Los Angeles, Calif.
Art Institute, Zanesville, Ohio
Bennington Museum, Vermont
Atlanta Art Association, Atlanta, Georgia
Shelburne Museum, Vermont

Musée National d'Art Moderne, Paris
Kunsthistorisches Museum, Vienna, Austria
National Gallery of New South Wales, Sydney, Australia
Queensland National Art Gallery, Brisbane, Australia
Oxford University, Great Britain
Pushkin Museum, Moscow, U.S.S.R.

Comments of European Papers

FRANCE

Arts, Paris—December 8, 1950

Grandma Moses, so-called primitive painter, is as famous in the United States as the greatest artists who are not primitives . . . The American enthusiasm for this lady can very well be understood . . . Few of these so-called primitive painters are actually capable of presenting a show of such quality . . . And it is a great pleasure to walk through such an exhibition, where the soul is devoted to the peaceful life in the quiet streets or in the warm interiors, in the midst of animals running loose or women working quietly. Thanks go to Grandma Moses for the happiness which she shows us.

Paris *Presse*—December 7, 1950

. . . Her art is sombre, direct and sometimes in her paintings, a corner of the sky, a group of people, evoke the greatest realistic painters of all times.

Le Monde, Paris—December 9, 1950

The serene sweetness of a daring old lady who makes the Americans of 1950 take pleasure in recognizing themselves in these simple and friendly images. It will also astonish many Europeans to discover these same qualities.

New York Herald Tribune, European Edition, Paris— Dec. 5, 1962

. . . Though naive in the best sense of the word, she was by no means a primitive. What strikes one is the sophistication with which she achieves certain effects. Her landscapes have depth, and the farawayness of distant blue mountains is beautifully conveyed. In "Shenandoah Valley" the landscape is composed of varied tones, while the river is rendered as a flat sheet of blue-gray which Whistler might have envied . . .

Claude Roger-Marx, *Le Figaro Litteraire,* Paris

. . . It is because no thought of fame or fortune ever touched her that these compositions present a characteristic authenticity, often missing in "Sunday painters" whose very success has turned them into "seven day painters". . . . Grandma Moses . . . asked advice only of the sky (the sky which Claude Monet said was the only teacher in painting). . . . Recapturing her own childhood through the deeds and gestures of her children and grandchildren, in her eyes the only important events—and those which make of her a true painter—are seasonal and atmospheric . . .

René Barotte, Paris *Presse*—November 27, 1962

. . . Never has an artist represented with greater truth each of the moments of rustic life. . . . Aside from certain lesser Dutch masters of the 17th century I know of no painter who has more poetically "wrapped" the world in snow or better sensed the coming of springtime . . .

Jean Francois Chabrun, *L'Express,* Paris—November 29, 1962

. . . That such an old woman should have been able to retain in her manner of looking at things, and of expressing them, the freshness of an admirably gifted young girl, this is what is so marvelous and so reassuring. And then, through her, it is a rustic and tender America which we discover. An America where whatever made Grandma Moses paint has nothing—absolutely nothing—in common with what makes Sammy run.

SWITZERLAND

Weltwoche, Zürich—Sept. 15, 1950

. . . The charming stories of Grandma Moses, her childlike portrayals of life on the farm, do not emanate from any literary striving toward "the simple life." She grasps the environment which she so well knows, with magic spontaneity. Her approach to nature is completely unsentimental and as untouched as nature herself. The fact that Grandma Moses exists and that she commands such universal attention, that too is a phenomenon of our times.

National Zeitung, Basle—Sept. 19, 1950

For quite some time already, magazines in great numbers, have brought us the fame of Grandma Moses. . . . As a rule, sensation does not become a creative force, and so there is something nice about the fact that after all the noise of the press, radio and the movies, one finally comes in contact with the art itself, so completely real, untouched, so autochthon. . . . Just because the art of Grandma Moses is so completely unromantic, our approach to it must be the same. She will be accepted as a phenomenon of nature, unique and irreproduceable.

GREAT BRITAIN

Art News and Review, London—April 28, 1956

. . . In the age of aesthetic confusion she has achieved *clarity;* she knows what she wants to do, and she does it with a pure, deft technique. She "sees" clearly, and she paints likewise, a fact that will distress only the hypocrite. So "artless" is her achievement that many will be inclined to dismiss it summarily—for all its naive charm—as basically shallow, brittle, or modish: time, I feel sure, will prove this snap judgment to be false . . . Age has nothing to do with the Grandma Moses case—nor has the fact that like Utrillo she never saw the inside of an art school. She is plainly and simply a painter with a needle-sharp eye for detail, and a facility for decorative organisation that is rivalled only by the painters of Persia and India. The poetic and mystic content of her art is closely linked with the springs of that eternal youthfulness which has preserved the Maytime of her childhood (and ours by implication), like gay butterflies in crystal amber. The snow falls, the wind blows, the train puffs, the horses tug, the cars chug, and the children play in this everlasting morning of life. For the preservation of this happy idyll we must be grateful to Grandma, though I know that there are some who will deny vehemently, that sheer, simple happiness is much of a justification for art. Set as it is amid the squalor and filth of modern materialism, the unashamed simplicity and bible-clean goodness of Grandma Moses' art is more likely to endure than the mishapen and demented ravings of the second generation of psychological and abstract painters.

The Times, London—April 18, 1956

. . . Two things especially distinguish her paintings—the subtlety of her tonality and the truth of their movement. Most Sunday painters depict a series of concepts, of separate things-in-themselves . . . The objects in Mrs. Moses' pictures cast no shadows, it is true, but mood and tone are none the less often very exact. It would not be easy, for example, to find passages from other primitive paintings comparable with that of the earliest picture shown here, "Sugaring Off," painted in 1939, of the little boy in the white woolly against the white snow; or of almost any of her distant mountains; or again, in what is perhaps her masterpiece here, "The Thunderstorm," of the piles of hay against the grassy ground. These are imagined whole, as a unity.

The Manchester *Guardian* Weekly—April 21, 1956

. . . It is easy to dismiss pictures which are as extremely pretty as these. But an unusual power of arrangement and organization is evident in some of them. There is a deep feeling for the American landscape . . .

AUSTRIA

Wiener *Zeitung,* Vienna—October 19, 1962

Whatever publicity about Grandma Moses has reached us before now is all at once forgotten the moment one comes under the spell of the exhibition of this unusual woman. Something magical begins to happen . . . when confronted with the originals for the first time, one is happily surprised. What delicacy of color-graduation . . . the great purity of this really not so "naive" painting has a magical effect, one is amazed at . . . the manner in which depth of a landscape is captured on the flat picture surface and by the color values of rolling hills in the blue distance. What the great landscape painters consciously composed, Grandma Moses "knew" from inborn sensitivity without knowledge of perspective and color . . .

Presse, Vienna—October 19, 1962

. . . Anyone who, like the critic of contemporary primitive art, tends to be somewhat skeptical, . . . will be surprised at how good a painter she was. She is essentially a primitive only when painting figures or animals . . . the landscapes, however, are precious paintings, recalling Camille Pissarro (sometimes even in the color selection) and are so full of devotion, and so steeped in interest in the mood of seasonal light changes, that Grandma Moses must be called a born painter.

Kleine Zeitung, Vienna—October 21, 1962

The Grandma Moses exhibition in Vienna is due to become this season's main event. One must imagine a painter of genius . . . through whom nature makes herself felt without distortion, in order to have an approximate criterion for the work of Grandma Moses . . . her talent must be considered as a natural phenomenon.

GERMANY

Hamburger *Abendblatt*—March 5, 1963

. . . Painting with such color and mood values is anything but primitive. These landscapes have an often astounding artistic beauty . . .

Bergedorfer Zeitung, Hamburg—March 12, 1963

. . . There is scarcely anything comparable . . . that arouses in the public so much wonder and delight. . . . (Grandma Moses) has become one of the best loved painters of the world.

Die Welt, Hamburg—March 12, 1963

. . . Her scenes—as lively as they are inviting—are filled with such pure naivete, wisdom and joie de vivre as one only seldom finds in so-called "primitives". . . . a very worthwhile exhibition.

Fuldauer *Volkszeitung*—May 11, 1963

. . . Grandma Moses is perhaps the most genuine phenomenon in American art. One would not do justice to her art in calling it genial. Untainted by the background of a . . . standard of established European artistic tradition, she created her pictures in splendid unencumbered naivete . . .

Ruhr-Nachrichten, Dortmund—June 22, 1963

. . . In 20 years she has created with her pictures one of the most precious national monuments of the American people, and given witness to all men of an unknown, hardworking life, one of the most admirable chapters in the book of the family of man.

Wiesbadner *Kurier*—August 5, 1963

. . . The most refreshing, youthful pictures one has ever seen. . . . she delights us with her magnificent legacy. She knew nothing of her originality as a painter, of her own unique Grandma Moses style. One will certainly avoid in the future calling her a primitive.

Berliner *Morgenpost*—October 25, 1963

The exhibition . . . offers a welcome opportunity to test the legend of Grandma Moses on its esthetic validity. It proves that the legend resists every such test: even more, it is identical with reality. . . . It is absolutely inconceivable not to leave the exhibition more cheerfully than upon going in . . .

Die Zeit, Hamburg—February 23, 1956

Though much has been written about Grandma Moses and her pictures, nothing can convey the ever fresh, naive charm that emanates from her paintings. Compared with the works of this aged American woman, the pictures of Henri Rousseau and the other "Sunday Painters" that follow in his footsteps seem classical, but there is an irresistible appeal in the carefree non-professional approach of Anny Mary Robertson Moses. If there is such a thing as a puritanical fairy-tale, it can be found in Grandma's pictures. She has no use for metaphysics, or even for dreams. All her life she has remained a farm wife. The secret of the effect produced by her pictures can probably be attributed in part to the simple relish she takes in story telling and in her joy of bright colors. She indulges in both with no thought of fashion and trend, they are to her merely an unreflected expression of life itself.

NORWAY, FINLAND, SWEDEN AND DENMARK

In these countries, too, the exhibition of Grandma Moses' works in 1960-64 was an unusual success. Glowing reviews appeared in the papers. It would be repetitive to quote excerpts from the extensive coverage of this show which was called "unusual," "extraordinary," "beautiful"; everywhere it attracted large attendances, and the public was fascinated with her works. In Oslo, 8000 persons visited the exhibition, among them, King Olav V, with princess Ragnhild. In Helsinki, the show "roused out-of-the-normal interest"; 6000 visitors were counted, and the catalogues were sold out, "borrowed copies had to be placed at the disposal of the visitors—an unusual event for Helsinki."

RUSSIA

In Moscow, an exhibition took place at the famous Pushkin Museum in 1964, upon the invitation by the U.S.S.R. Ministry for Culture.

From a letter by the Counselor for Cultural Affairs of the United States Embassy in Moscow:

. . . The show was very well received by the public, once they had overcome their initial surprise. Judging by the comments we heard at the Museum or from Soviet acquaintances who had seen it, the evident delight that Grandma Moses took in the execution of all her work was the most impressive aspect for the Soviets. They were surprised, and quite pleased, to find a total absence of "social message". . . . No figures were kept on attendance. The Pushkin is a very large museum which gets many visitors. I would judge that 100,000 viewers would not be too generous an estimate. And it is true there were lines of people waiting to see it on several occasions. . . . The Embassy regards the Moses exhibit as a successful and very valid effort in the campaign to increase Soviet understanding of the United States and its people . . .

FROM LETTERS

. . . By actions such as the Grandma Moses exhibition, the people of the two countries . . . learn to understand the spirit and philosophy of their respective inhabitants.

A. N. HOPMAN, *Head of U. S. Information Centers in Austria.*

The Grandma Moses exhibition was a great success; it had more visitors per day than any exhibition before. . . . I believe that this exhibition brought more good will for America than any other single effort we have made here.

H. B. SIEMER, *Senior Representative, Information Services Branch, Salzburg*

The Grandma Moses exhibition has been a great success here as far as the interpretation of American culture is concerned. Because her paintings have no European influence, they have been particularly effective.

DONALD DUNHAM, *Press and Cultural Attache Legation of the United States of America, Berne*

The exhibition was an extraordinary success. We had 2500 paying visitors and 800 members and artists who pay no admission. These figures mean very much for a three weeks' period. . . . I was very sorry that we could not have an extension of the show.

M. RUEDLINGER, *Director Kunsthalle, Berne.*

The exhibition of Grandma Moses enjoys an extraordinary success, expressing itself in the many visitors we daily receive and the great attention the press pays to it.

K. E. SCHUURMAN, *Curator Gemeentemuseum, The Hague*

THE WHITE HOUSE
WASHINGTON

May 26, 1949

Dear Grandma Moses:

I certainly appreciated your good letter of May twenty-third. I am glad you enjoyed your visit to Washington.

Mrs. Truman and I were delighted to see you at the dinner and to have you at the Blair House for tea. My piano playing doesn't amount to much but I am glad you enjoyed it.

I hope you have many, many happy years ahead of you.

Sincerely yours,

Harry Truman

Mrs. Anna Mary Robertson Moses
Eagle Bridge
New York

Letter of President Truman, May 26, 1949

Eagle Bridge new york.

Dear Sir Winston Churchill

I am really sorry that you stepped aside, because I always felt safe while you were the Prime minister of England,

But we all have to step down sooner or later,

I know you won't be idle you have your painting, and it is a lovely hobby for us older people,

I wish you long life good health and happiness,

Grandma Moses,

April 6 1955,

Letter to Sir Winston Churchill, April 6, 1955

Grandma Moses
Eagle Bridge
New York

Jan. 12 1956.

Mr. President,

I was very honored to be asked to paint a picture of your home in Gettysburg.

although most of my paintings are memories and imagination, I tried to do this for you and hope it will please you.

my very best wishes for your Continued good health on your third anniversary, as our President.

Very sincerely,
Grandma moses,

Letter to President Eisenhower, Jan. 12, 1956

THE WHITE HOUSE

WASHINGTON

January 18, 1956

Dear Grandma Moses:

Mrs. Eisenhower and I are truly delighted with your interesting and imaginative conception of our Gettysburg farm. Your painting, presented by the members of the Cabinet on the third anniversary of my Inauguration, will be, I know, one of the great treasures of the Eisenhower family.

With the deep appreciation of Mrs. Eisenhower and myself come also our good wishes to you for many more years of happiness and health,

Sincerely,

Dwight D. Eisenhower

Grandma Moses
Eagle Bridge
New York

Letter from President Eisenhower, Jan. 18, 1956

P R O C L A M A T I O N

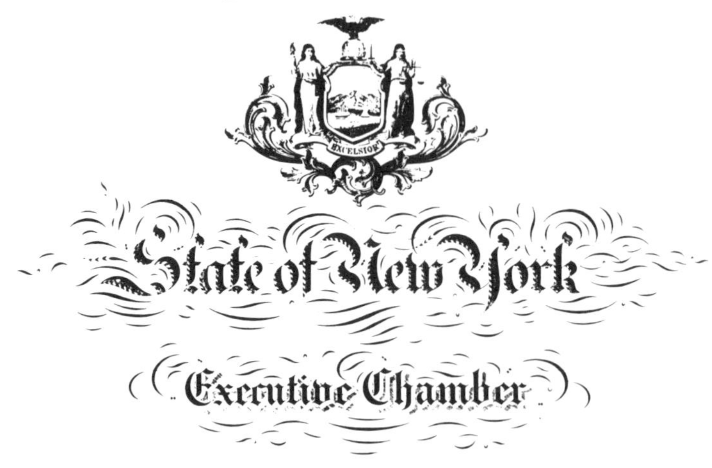

One year before the beginning of the Civil War a little girl destined for unique achievement and renown, was born "back in the green meadows and wild woods on a farm in Washington County, New York." The quotation is in her own words. Her name today is Anna Mary Robertson Moses. We all admire and love her as Grandma Moses.

For three score years and ten she carried on the work of a farmer's wife and mother of eleven children.

Then, as she puts it herself, she started to paint in her old age, although she had previously painted "little pictures for Christmas gifts and things like that."

Everybody knows what happened with the canvases that Mrs. Moses created for her own pleasure. The world, in Emerson's words, "beat a path to her door." There is no more renowned artist in our entire country today.

So it becomes us, the people of the Empire State, to salute Grandma Moses on the occasion of her one-hundred and first birthday.

NOW, THEREFORE, I, Nelson A. Rockefeller, Governor of the State of New York, do hereby proclaim September 7, 1961, as

GRANDMA MOSES DAY

in New York State.

G I V E N under my hand and the Privy Seal of the State at the Capitol in the City of Albany this twenty-first day of August in the year of our Lord one thousand nine hundred and sixty-one.

Nelson Rockefeller

BY THE GOVERNOR

Secretary to the Governor

Proclamation by Governor Rockefeller, September, 1961

THE WHITE HOUSE

WASHINGTON

September 5, 1961

Dear Grandma Moses:

I want again to send you my warmest best wishes as you reach another milestone in your long and celebrated career.

Your painting and your personal influence continue to play a large and valuable role in our national life.

Both Mrs. Kennedy and I want to wish you best health and happiness in the years ahead.

Sincerely,

Grandma Moses
Eagle Bridge, New York

Letter from President Kennedy, Sept. 5, 1961, on the occasion of the artist's 101st birthday

Her paintings are a pure delight, cool and sunny and clear as a Mason jar full of spring water.

—*Archibald MacLeish*

The directness and vividness of her paintings restored a primitive freshness to our own perception of the American scene. Both her work and her life helped our nation renew its pioneer heritage and recalled its roots in the country-side and on the frontier.

—*John F. Kennedy*

DOCUMENTARY MATERIAL IN THE BENNINGTON MUSEUM

**Asterisk Denotes Illustration in This Volume*

I. Grandma Moses' "Tip-Up" Table, which she used as an "easel" for many years. Its base is covered with six very early paintings.* (See "My Tip-Up Table.")

Grandma Moses' chair, used at the above table. *Both lent by Mrs. Hugh W. Moses.*

II. PHOTOGRAPHS

a) The artist's mother, Mary Shanahan Robertson, at the age of twenty-four.
b) The artist's father, Russell King Robertson, about 1860.
c) Anna Mary Robertson, four years old. *
d) Anna Mary Robertson Moses as bride, 1887. *
e) Thomas Salmon Moses as bridegroom, 1887. *
f) Grandma Moses with two of her children, about 1903. *
g) Grandma Moses with two of her great-grandchildren, 1949. *
h) Grandma Moses, painting, 1946.
i) President Harry S. Truman presenting to Grandma Moses the Women's National Press Club Award "for outstanding accomplishment in art." Washington, D. C., 1949.
j) Grandma Moses, seated at her "Tip-Up" Table, interviewed by Edward R. Murrow, 1955. *
k) Grandma Moses, painting, 1955. *
l) Grandma Moses on her 101st birthday, September 7, 1961. *
m) The hands of Grandma Moses. *
n) Top of the artist's painting table. *
o) Grandma Moses' bedroom. *

III. PORTRAITS OF GRANDMA MOSES

a) George Daniel Hoffman: Grandma Moses. Oil on masonite. 1949.
b) Boris Chaliapin: Portrait of Grandma Moses. Original for the cover of *Time* Magazine, December 28, 1953. Autograph of Grandma Moses on the mat.

IV. DOCUMENTS
Photostats

a) Composition, written by Anna Mary Robertson for the last day of school, about 1874.
b) Wedding Certificate of Anna Mary Robertson and Thomas Salmon Moses, 1887.
c) Grandma Moses' account of the first Christmas she remembers, written in 1952.
d) Two pages from the artist's "Record Book." Example of labels which the artist pasted on the back of most of her paintings. *
e) Society of Mayflower Descendants: 1) The election of Grandma Moses to membership. 2) Citation.
f) Women's National Press Club Award. Presented to Grandma Moses by President Harry S. Truman, Washington, D. C. 1949. *
g) Letters and telegrams sent to Grandma Moses by President Harry S. Truman. *
h) Card with reproduction of a painting by General Dwight D. Eisenhower, sent to Grandma Moses from France, 1952.
i) Telegram and letters sent to Grandma Moses by President Dwight D. Eisenhower.
j) Letter to Grandma Moses from President John F. Kennedy. *
k) Letter to Grandma Moses and two Proclamations by Governor Nelson A. Rockefeller, dated September 7, 1960 and September 7, 1961, proclaiming this, the artist's birthday as "Grandma Moses Day" in New York State. *
l) Letter to Grandma Moses from Vice-President Richard M. Nixon.
m) Letter to Grandma Moses from Governor Adlai E. Stevenson.
n) Letters and telegrams sent to Grandma Moses by President Herbert Hoover, Governor Averell Harriman, Governor Nelson A. Rockefeller, Senator Kenneth B. Keating, Senator Jacob K. Javits, Mayor Robert F. Wagner, Lillian Gish, Douglas Fairbanks, Jr., and others.
o) Letter from Grandma Moses to Prime Minister Sir Winston Churchill. *
p) Letter from Grandma Moses to President Dwight D. Eisenhower.
q) Facsimile of Grandma Moses' handwritten "Thank-you-card" on her 95th birthday, 1955.

V. PAINTING TABLE SUPPLIES AND RELATED OBJECTS

a) Brushes.
b) Jars, bottle tops and jar tops of various sizes on which the artist

mixed her colors.
c) Tubes of paint.
d) Pieces of cloth.
e) Sewing and embroidering supplies.
f) First phase of a worsted picture.
g) Tray.
h) Calendar of 1952.
i) Model of a pump made for Grandma Moses by a friend, about 1950.
j) Mittens knitted by Grandma Moses of wool left over from worsted pictures.

VI. POSTERS

a) Grandma Moses' first exhibition, Galerie St. Etienne, New York, 1940.
b) Neue Galerie, Vienna, 1950. (First Grandma Moses exhibition in Europe.)
c) Kunsthalle Bern, 1950.
d) Gemeentemuseum, The Hague, 1950.
e) Services des relations culturelles de l'Ambassade des Etats Unis, Paris, 1950.
f) Exhibition shown in ten museums in Austria and Germany, 1962-64.
g) Svenska Handelsbanken, Stockholm, 1964.
h) Louisiana Museum, Copenhagen, 1964.
i) *My Life's History* by Grandma Moses, 1952. Poster for the book.

VII. BOOKS BY AND ABOUT GRANDMA MOSES
(Selection)
a) *Grandma Moses: American Primitive.* Edited by Otto Kallir. Introduction by Louis Bromfield. First edition: Dryden Press, New York, 1946. Second edition: Doubleday & Co., Garden City, 1947.
b) *Christmas* by Grandma Moses, facsimile, 1952.
c) *My Life's History* by Grandma Moses. Edited by Otto Kallir. Harper & Row, New York, 1952. Andre Deutsch, London 1952. German edition: *Meine Lebensgeschichte.* Ullstein Verlag, 1957. Dutch edition: *Het verhaal van mijn leven.* A. W. Bruna & Zoon, 1958.
d) *The Grandma Moses Storybook.* Stories and poems by 28 writers. Illustrated by Grandma Moses. Edited by Nora Kramer. Biographical sketch of Grandma Moses by Otto Kallir. Random House, New York, 1961.
e) *The Night Before Christmas* by Clement C. Moore. With pictures especially painted for this book by Grandma Moses. Random House, New York, 1961.

VIII. CATALOGUES, CLIPPINGS, MAGAZINES

a) Sheet of clippings from reviews of the first one-man show of paintings by Grandma Moses, Galerie St. Etienne, New York, October

1940.

b) Invitation to the first Grandma Moses exhibition in Europe, Vienna 1950.

c) Selected catalogues of Grandma Moses exhibitions that took place in the United States and Europe.

d) Selected newspaper clippings about Grandma Moses.

e) Selected newspaper clippings on the death of Grandma Moses.

f) Selected magazines from-all over the world with covers by Grandma Moses and feature articles.

IX. MUSIC

a) *The Grandma Moses Suite,* by Hugh Martin, orchestrated by Alec Wilder. Columbia Records. Music composed for the color film on Grandma Moses' life and work. Photography by Erica Anderson, narration by Archibald MacLeish, directed by Jerome Hill.

b) *Down In the Valley,* by Kurt Weill. Record: RCA Victor. Cover by Grandma Moses. Score: G. Schirmer, Inc. New York. Cover by Grandma Moses.

c) *Christmas with Grandma Moses.* Christmas music with commentary spoken by Grandma Moses. Many paintings, photographs and quotations from the artist's writings in the descriptive booklet bound into the record album. RCA Victor.

d) *Christmas Organ and Chimes.* Diplomat Christmas Records. Cover by Grandma Moses.

e) *Storia della musica: La musica in America.* Fratelli Fabbri Editori (Italy). Reproduction of Grandma Moses painting in descriptive booklet.

f) *La musica moderna.* Fratelli Fabbri Editori. Cover and reproductions in descriptive booklet by Grandma Moses.

X. CHRISTMAS CARDS

a) The first Grandma Moses Christmas cards, 1946: Box, autographed on top by the artist, containing sixteen different cards.

b) Hallmark Christmas cards, published over a period of many years: Selected boxes, single cards, notecards.

c) Christmas cards, notecards, postcards, published in Germany.

d) Christmas card published in England.

XI. MISCELLANEOUS

a) "Easy Apply Mural," in four parts, reproducing the painting *Williamstown* by Grandma Moses.

b) Fabrics on which paintings by Grandma Moses have been reproduced.

c) Ceramic tiles on which designs are reproduced that were painted by Grandma Moses for this purpose.

d) Round tiles framed in wooden plates, showing reproductions of paintings by Grandma Moses.

e) Hand-printed kerchief, made in Austria.

Illustrations

CATALOGUE OF THE EXHIBITION

FROM THE GRANDMA MOSES GALLERY AT THE BENNINGTON MUSEUM, BENNINGTON VERMONT

Most of the pictures by Grandma Moses were painted in oil and tempera on cardboard or masonite. Other media are specifically mentioned.

Dimensions are given in inches. Height precedes width.

**Asterisk denotes illustration in this volume.*

When comments on pictures are printed in italics, they are quotations from the writings of Grandma Moses.

EARLIEST PICTURES

before the artist started numbering and dating her work.

1. FIREBOARD, ca. 1920. 32 x 39. Oil on paper. *
2. VILLAGE IN WINTER. 8 x 10. Signed. *
3. THE FIRST AUTOMOBILE. 9¾ x 11½. Signed. *
4. BRINGING IN THE HAY. 13½ x 22. Signed.
5. GOING TO TOWN. 10 1/8 x 8 1/8. Signed.
6. FIRE IN THE WOODS. 10¼ x 15. Signed.
7. THE GUARDIAN ANGEL. 9 x 7. Signed.
8. CHOPPING WOOD FOR THE MINISTER. 11½ x 9¾. Signed.
9. MILLER IN THE DELL. 9½ x 11½. Signed.
10. HUNTMAN'S DREAM. 11½ x 13½. Signed.
11. DOWN IN THE GLEN. 10¾ x 13¾.
12. WATERFALLS, 14 x 22. *
13. CAMBRIDGE IN THE VALLEY. 15½ x 22½.
14. THE COVERED WAGON. 11 x 14. Signed.
15. APPLE PICKERS. 13 x 12½.
16. AT THE OLD WELL. 14 x 14. Oil on canvas.
17. FARM ALONG THE RIVER. 15 x 17¼. Signed.

18. THE SHENANDOAH VALLEY–painting in two parts–both signed, 19¾ x 13¾ and 20¼ x 16¼. *
19. OLD HOMESTEAD. 9¼ x 11. Worsted picture. Signed.
20. OLD CASTLE ON A LAKE. 9 x 12. Worsted picture. Signed.
21. ROADSIDE GARDEN. 9½ x 16½. Worsted picture. *
22. SUNSET IN VIRGINIA. 11 x 14. Worsted picture.
23. WHEN THE SHEPHERD COMES FROM THE HILLS. 8¾ x 10½. Worsted picture. *
24. AUTUMN IN THE BERKSHIRES. 9 x 21¾. Worsted picture. Signed. *
25. CATCHING THE TURKEY. 12 x 16. Signed. *
26. THE OLD HOOSICK BRIDGE. 10 x 14. Worsted picture. Signed. *
27. AUTUMN IN THE BERKSHIRES. 8 x 14¼. Oil on canvas.
28. WASH DAY. 9¼ x 11¼.

PICTURES

with labels, mostly handwritten by Grandma Moses, giving number, title and date.

29. WHEN THE COWS COME HOME, 1941. 8¼ x 15¼. Signed. (GM 214).
30. FARM IN AUTUMN, 1941. 13 x 27. Signed. (GM 222).
31. SHEEP IN PASTURE, 1941. 8½ x 21½. Signed. (GM 2010!).
32. CAMBRIDGE VALLEY, 1942. 23½ x 27. Signed. (GM 234). *
33. BELVEDERE 1890, 1942. 22½ x 26½. Signed. (GM 303). *
34. OVER THE RIVER TO GRANDMA'S HOUSE, 1944. 17 x 26. Signed. (GM 525). *
35. BROTHER'S HOME, 1944. 12½ x 19 3/4. Signed. (GM 586).
36. IN THE PARK, 1944. 35½ x 44½. Signed. (GM 600). *
37. FIRST WAGON ON CAMBRIDGE PIKE, 1944. 20 x 24. Signed. (GM 793). *
38. EARLY SPRING TIME ON THE FARM, 1945. 16 x 25½. Signed. (GM 1026). *
39. IN HARVEST TIME, 1945. 18 x 28½. Signed. (GM 1057). *
40. BENNINGTON, 1945. 17¾ x 26. Signed. (GM 1088). *
41. HERE COMES AUNT JUDITH, 1946. 18 x 22¾. Signed. (GM 1098). *
42. POND IN FALL, 1946. 27 x 21. Signed. (GM 1159).
43. MARY AND LITTLE LAMB, 1947. 24 x 34¾. Signed. (GM 1161). *
44. APPLE-BUTTER MAKING, 1947. 19½ x 23¼. Signed. (GM 1165). *
45. WILLIAMSTOWN, 1947. 22 x 36. (GM 1167). *
46. TOM TOM PIPER'S SON, 1947. 15¾ x 20. Signed. (GM 1215). *
47. FOLLOW ME, 1948. 20 x 16. Signed. (GM 1236).
48. A BEAUTIFUL WORLD, 1948. 20 x 24. (GM 1286).
49. YEAR 1860–YEAR 1940, 1948. 26 x 21. Signed. (GM 1347-1348).*
THE SCHOOLHOUSE, 1949. 21 x 25. Signed. (GM 1364). Lent by Mrs. Hugh W. Moses.*

50. THE QUILTING BEE, 1950. 19¾ x 24. Signed. (GM 1374). *
51. THE OLD OAKEN BUCKET IN WINTER, 1950. 20 x 24. Signed. (GM 1408).*
52. THE OLD CHECKERED HOUSE (WINTER), 1950. 20 x 24. Signed. (GM 1409). *
53. DORSET, 1950. 19¾ x 24½. Signed. (GM 1413).
54. THE RANCH, 1950. 19 x 24. Signed. (GM 1414).
55. THE BARN DANCE, 1950. 35½ x 45. Oil on Canvas. Signed. (GM 1416). *
56. CANDLE-DIP DAY IN 1800, 1950. 9 x 9¼. Signed. (GM 1437). *
57. PODUNK, 1950. 26 x 32. (GM 1450).
58. THE POND, 1950. 18½ x 23½. Signed. (GM 1452).
59. MOVING DAY, 1951. 17 x 22. Signed. (GM 1456). *
60. THE FAMILY PICNIC, 1951. 17 x 22. Signed. (GM 1457).
61. THE DEPARTURE, 1951. 17½ x 22. Signed. (GM 1460). *
62. IT SNOWS, OH IT SNOWS, 1951. 24 x 30. Signed. (GM 1462). *
63. A FROSTY DAY, 1951. 18 x 24. Signed. (GM 1474). *
64. MOSES, 1953. 17½ x 24. Signed. (GM 1555). *
65. THE BATTLE OF BENNINGTON, 1953. 18 x 29¾. Signed. (GM 1590). *
66. SUGARING, 1955. 11 x 16. Signed. (GM 1679). *
67. EISENHOWER HOME, 1956. 16 x 24. Signed. (GM 1697). *
68. BLIZZARD, 1956. 16 x 24. Signed. (GM 1738). *
69. WIND STORM, 1956. 16 x 24. Signed. (GM 1739). *
70. TANDEM, 1956. 16 x 24. Signed. (GM 1741).
71. BALLOON, 1957. 16 x 24. Signed. (GM 1780). *
72. A BLIZZARD, 1958. 16 x 24. Signed. (GM 1833).
73. EAGLE BRIDGE HOTEL, 1959. 16 x 24. Signed. (GM 1864). *
74. BUSY TIME, 1959. 16 x 24. Signed. (GM 1904).

The following paintings were done by Grandma Moses as illustrations to "The Night Before Christmas" by Clement C. Moore. Published by Random House, New York, 1961.

75. SANTA CLAUS I, 1960. 16 x 23¾. Signed. (GM 1939). *
76. HERE COMES SANTA CLAUS, 1960. 12 x 16. Signed. (GM 1947).
77. SANTA CLAUS IS HERE, 1960. 16 x 24. Signed. (GM 1948).
78. NIGHT BEFORE CHRISTMAS, 1960. 12 x 16. Signed. (GM 1951). *
79. WAITING FOR SANTA CLAUS, 1960. 12 x 16. Signed. (GM 1952). *
80. JOLLY OLD SANTA, 1960. 12 x 16. Signed. (GM 1954).
81. YOU BETTER BE GOOD, 1960. 12 x 16. Signed. (GM 1955).

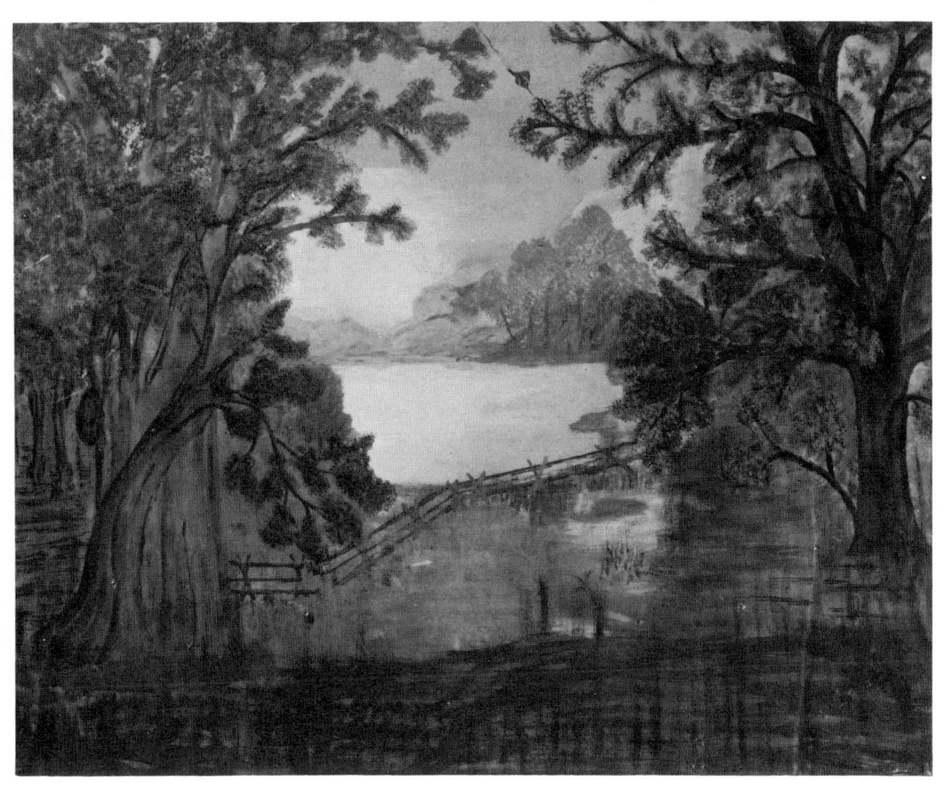

1

FIRE BOARD PAINTING
ca. 1920

One time I was papering the parlor, and I ran short of paper for the fire board. So I took a piece of paper and pasted it over the board, and I painted it a solid color first, then I painted two large trees on each side of it, like butternut trees. And back in it I did a little scene of a lake and painted it a yellow color, really bright, as though you were looking off into the sunlight. After three or four years, we re-papered the parlor and papered over the picture. When we re-papered the room again a few years ago, my daughter-in-law, Dorothy, remembered the picture, and we took the paper off the fire board, but the colors had faded somewhat. That was my first large picture.

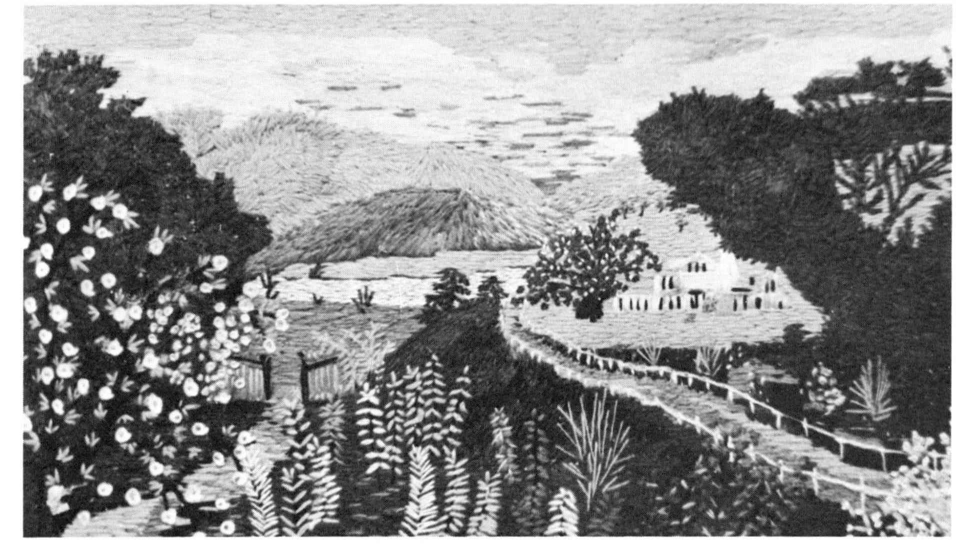

21 THE ROADSIDE GARDEN
Worsted Picture. Ca. 1939

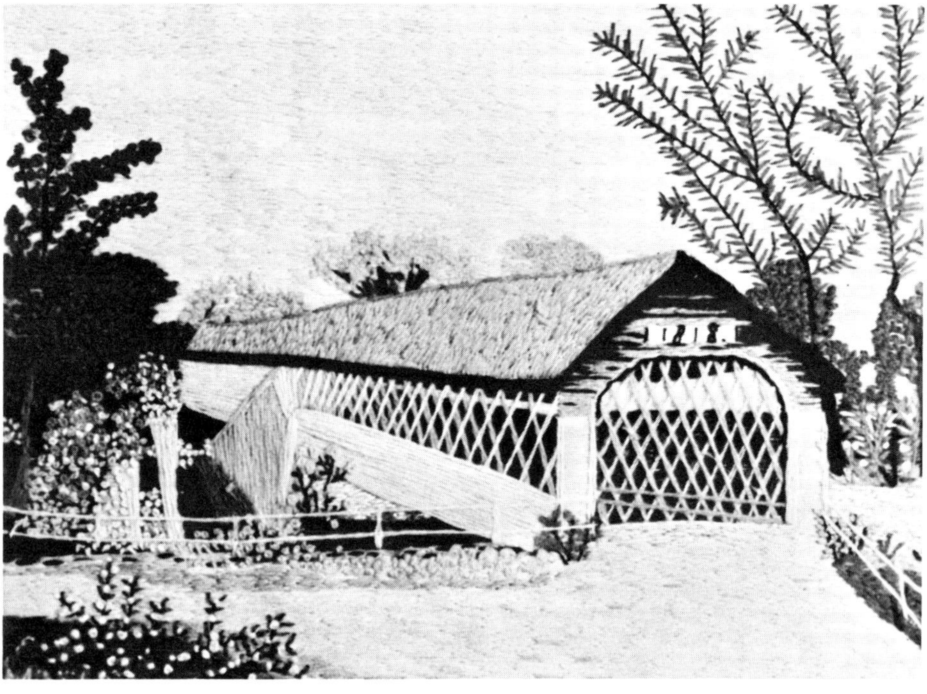

26 THE OLD HOOSICK BRIDGE
Worsted Picture. Ca. 1939

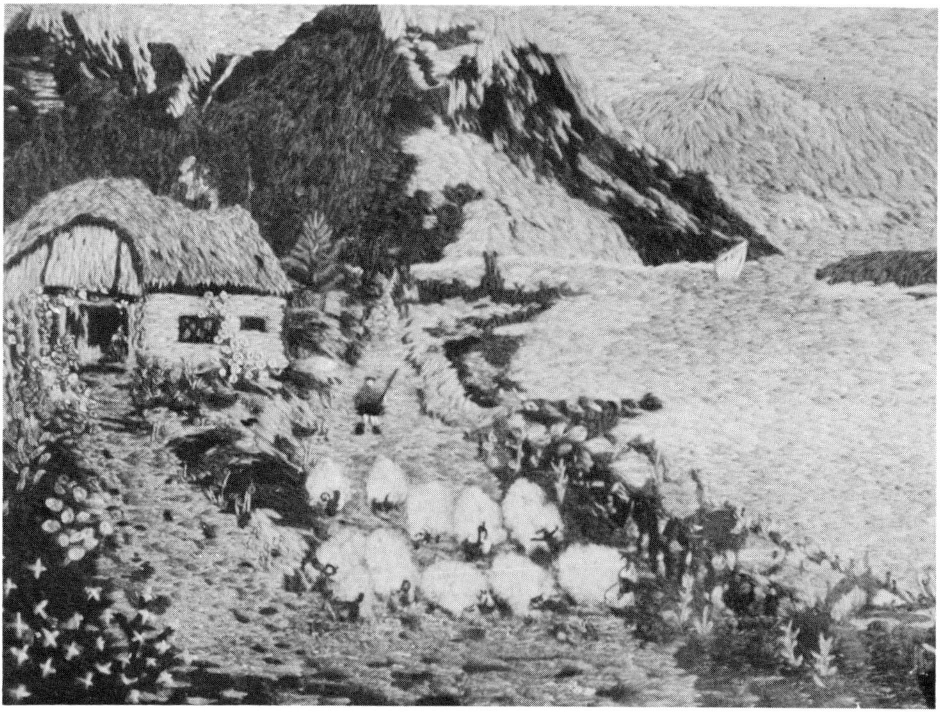

23 WHEN THE SHEPHERDS COME HOME
Worsted Picture. Ca. 1939

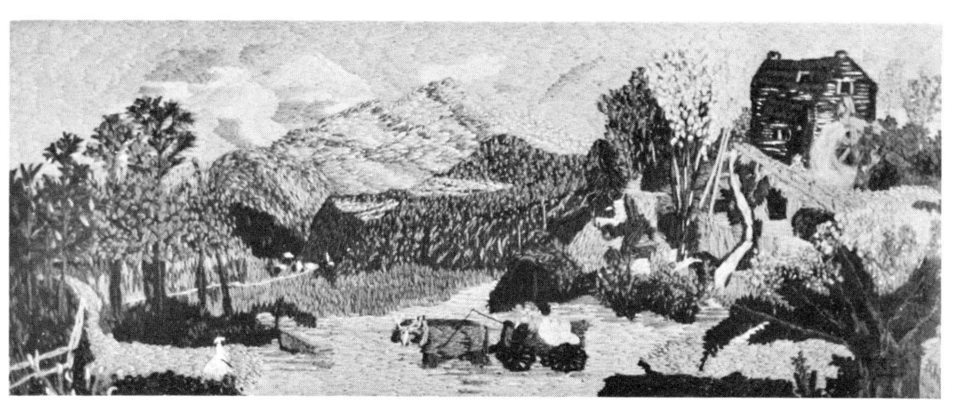

24 AUTUMN IN THE BERKSHIRES
Worsted Picture. Ca. 1939

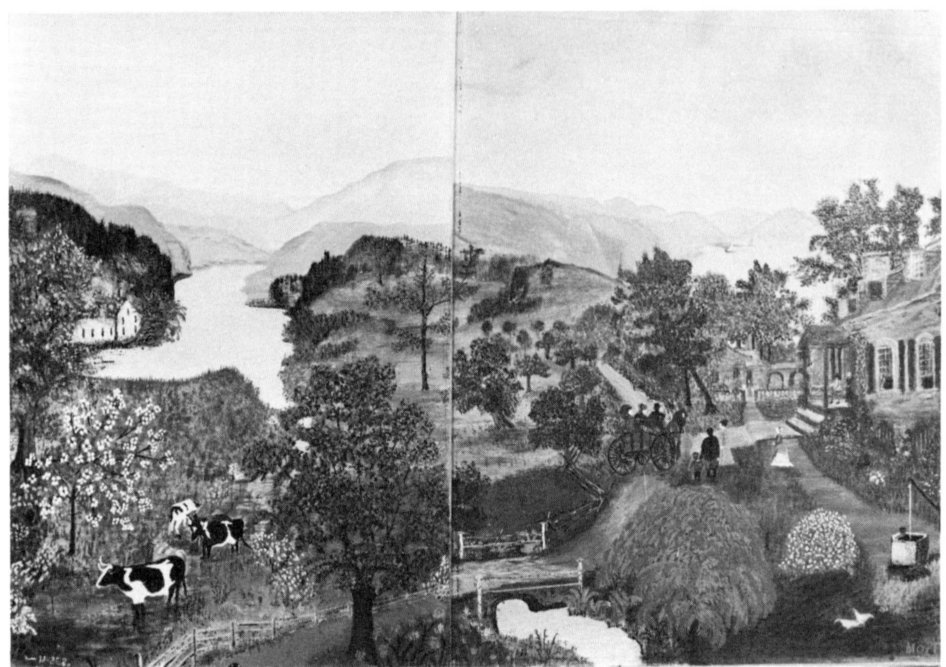

18

SHENANDOAH VALLEY
ca. 1939

These are the famous paintings which played an important role in the discovery of Grandma Moses' work. She wrote in her autobiography:

And then, one day, a Mr. Louis J. Caldor of New York City, an engineer and art collector, passing through the town of Hoosick Falls, saw and bought my paintings. He wanted to know who had painted them, and they told him it was an old woman that was living down on the Cambridge Road by the name of Anna Mary Moses. So when I came home that night, Dorothy said: "If you had been here, you could have sold all your paintings, there was a man here looking for them. I told him how many you had." She thought I had about ten, something like that.

Well, I didn't sleep much that night, I tried to think where I had any paintings and what they were, I knew I didn't have many, they were mostly worsted, but I thought, towards morning, of a painting I had started on after house cleaning days, when I found an old canvas and frame, and I thought I had painted a picture on it of Virginia. It was quite large, and I thought if I could find frames in the morning I could cut them right in two and make two pictures for him when he came. I did it so it wouldn't get Dorothy in the dog house. But he didn't discover the one I had cut in two for about a year, then he wanted to know what made me cut my best picture in two. I told him, it's just Scotch thrift.

The two pictures were part of the first Grandma Moses exhibition which took place at the Galerie St. Etienne in October 1940. At that time nobody paid much attention to the paintings, and one was later sold.

After Grandma Moses had become famous, efforts were made, unsuccessfully, to locate the sold half. In 1967 this missing section was brought to the Galerie St. Etienne and thus the two could be reunited.

It is interesting to observe that Grandma Moses not only cut the large painting into two parts to get the ten pictures ready for Mr. Caldor, but that she also added many details to the left half, in order to make it more complete, and then she signed it too. While the trees in the middleground and traces of the upper fence in the foreground show the former unity of the painting, a large tree was added to the picture on the left, as well as mountains in the background. The freshness of that painting is partly due to this later re-working by the artist, partly to its preservation under glass for almost thirty years, while the sold half has darkened somewhat because it was exposed to light and air without protection.

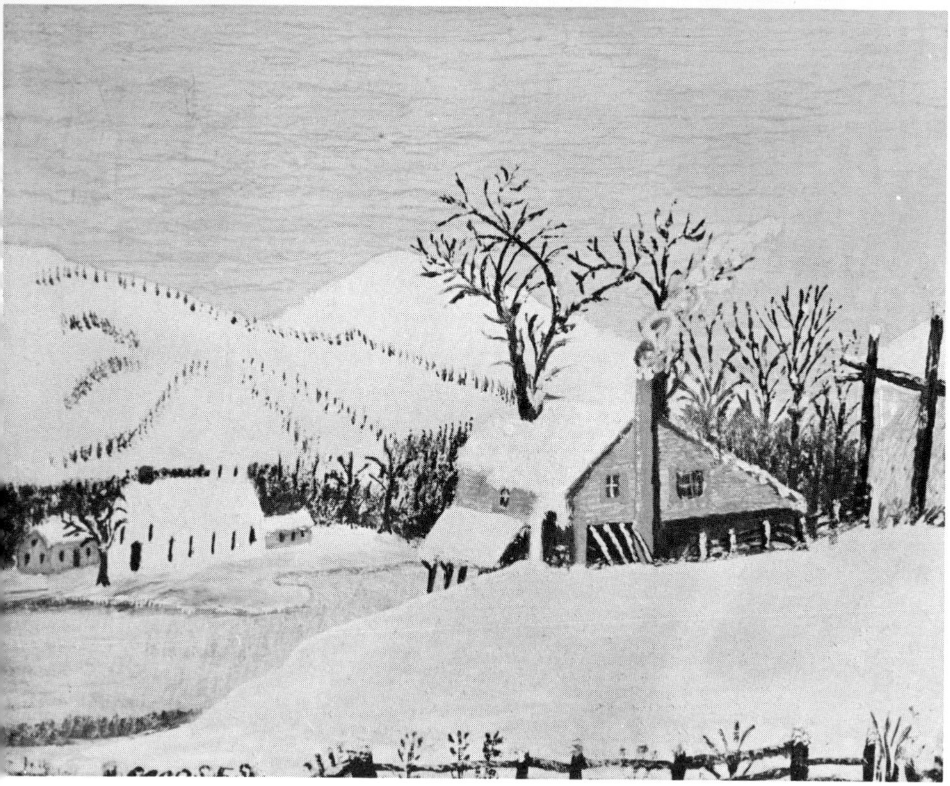

2

VILLAGE IN WINTER
Ca. 1939

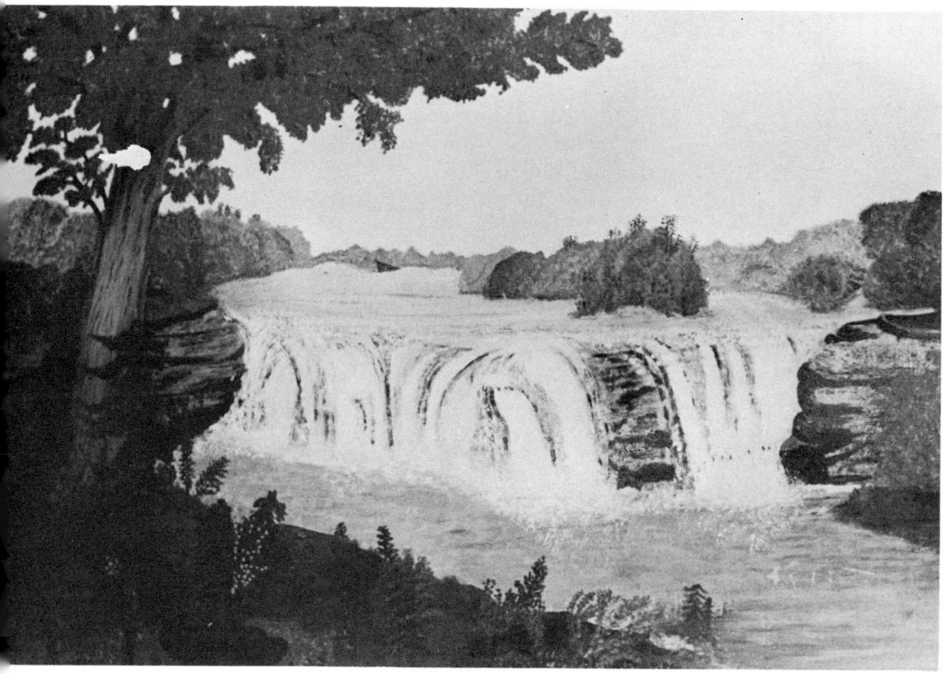

2

THE WATERFALLS
Ca. 1939

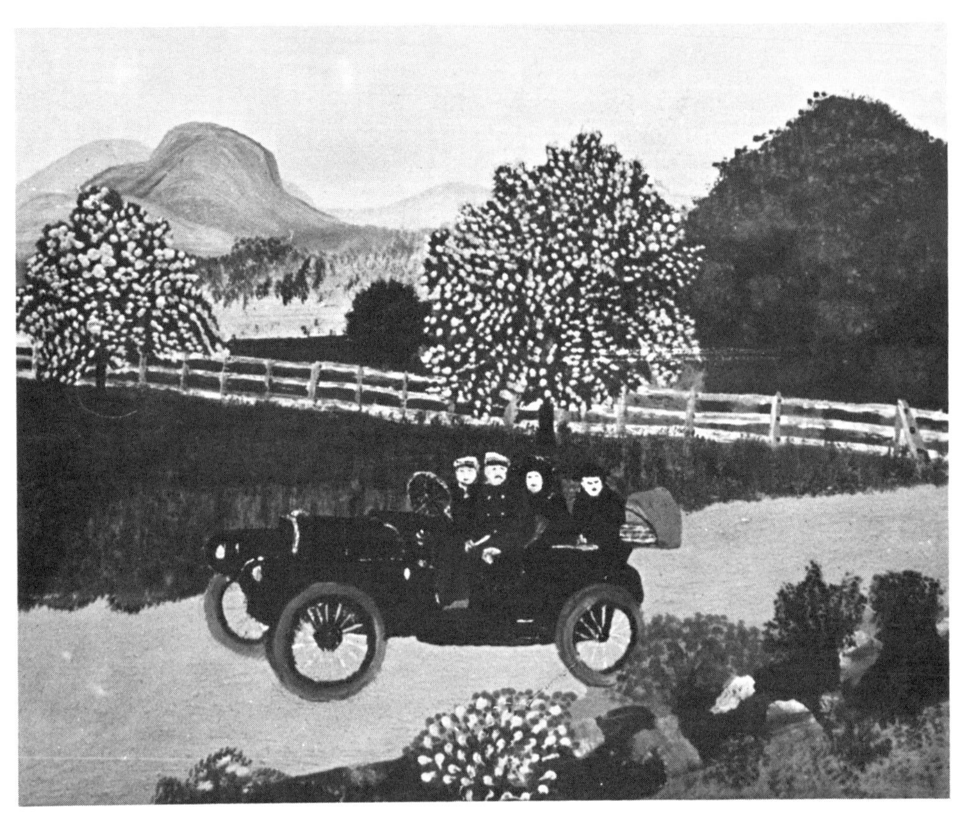

3

THE FIRST AUTOMOBILE
ca. 1939

Near Staunton, Virginia, I saw my first automobile. It was as high as it was long. It was owned by a Mr. Hausburger. He would take his wife and child for a ride going from Staunton down the pike to Harper's Ferry on a Sunday afternoon. The next one I saw, a Dr. Waite had. He had come back from the West to his home town and brought the car with him in 1909. But soon they were very plentiful, and now in a way they are a necessity.

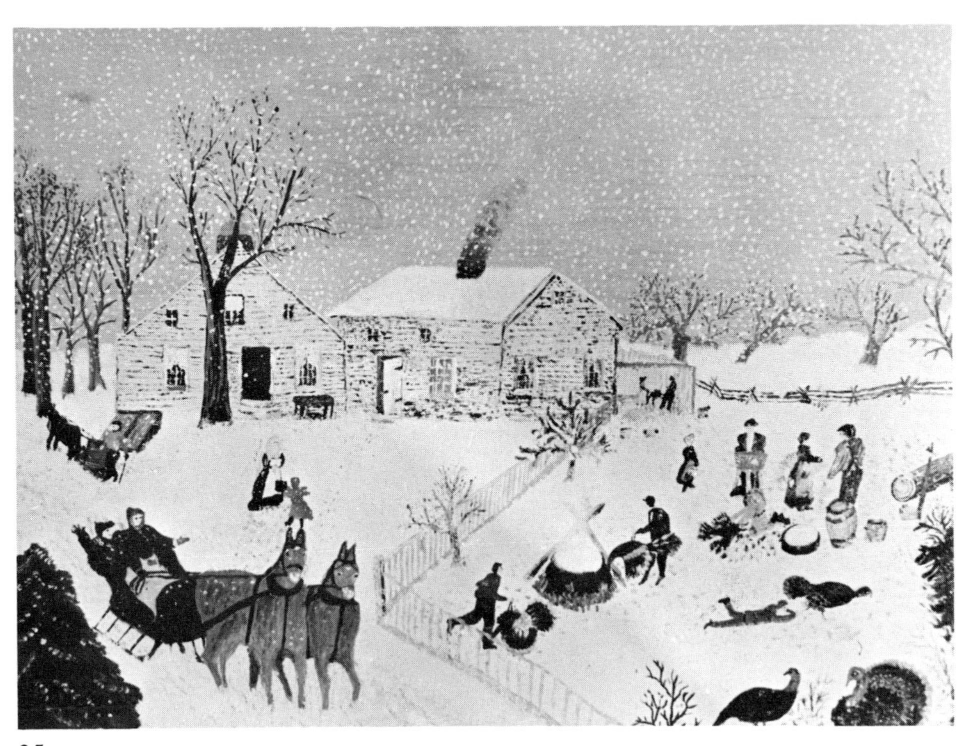

25

CATCHING THE THANKSGIVING TURKEY
1940

Why do we think we must have turkey for Thanksgiving?
Just because our forefathers did; they had it because turkeys were plentiful, and they did not have other kinds of meat. Now we have abundance of other kinds of luxuries.
Poor turkey, he has but one life to give to his country.

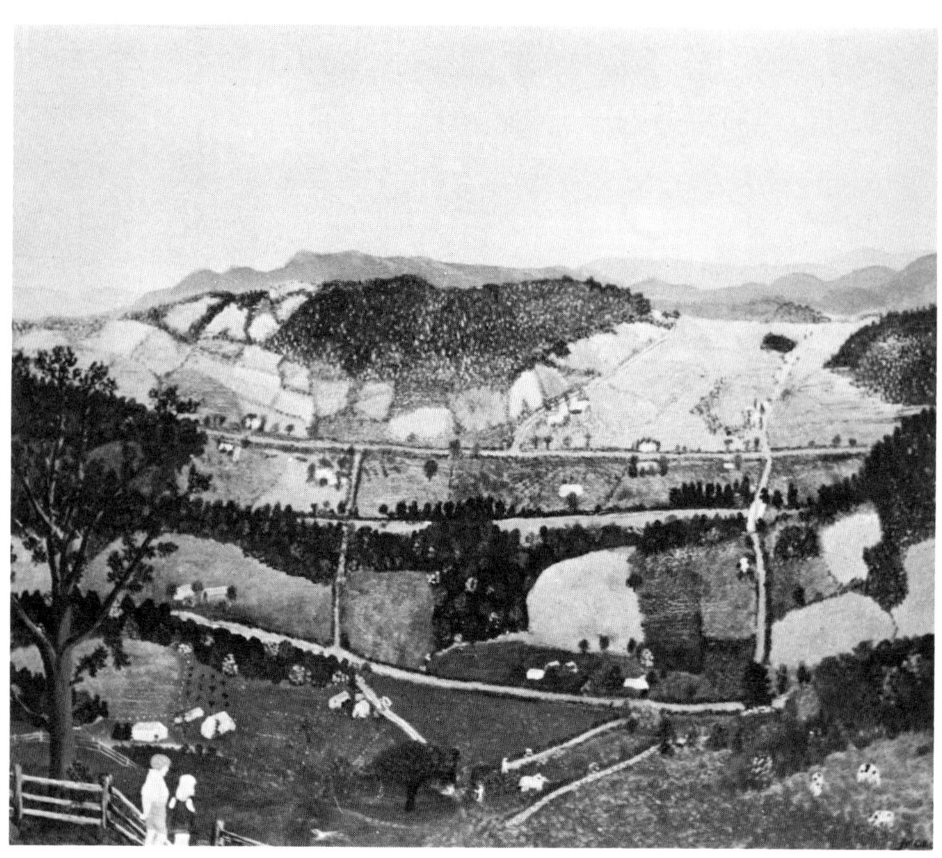

32

CAMBRIDGE VALLEY
1942

My ancestors were early settlers in Cambridge. My great-grandfather on my father's side, Hezekiah King, was born in Amenia, Duchess County, New York, 1775. When he was about twenty years old, he left his home and travelled into the Cambridge Valley, looking for a place in the wilderness, where he might build his future home, and there he cleared land and built him a house about 1778.

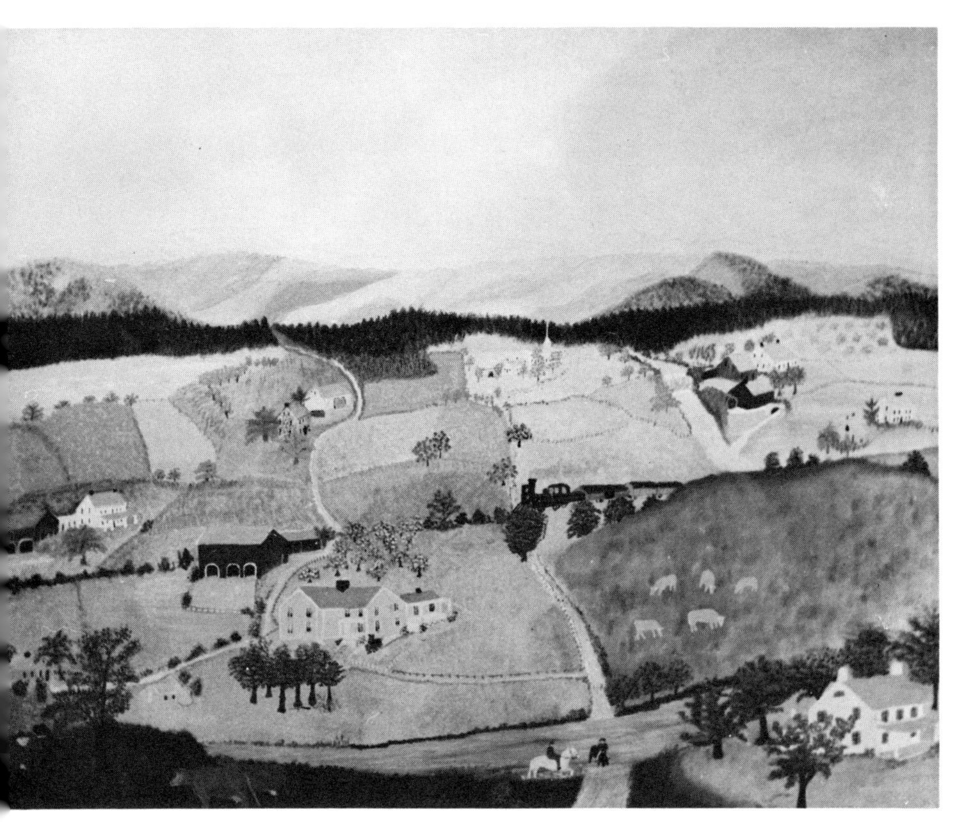

3

BELVEDERE 1890

The home of Grandma Moses for a few years while she was living in Virginia, in the Shenandoah Valley.

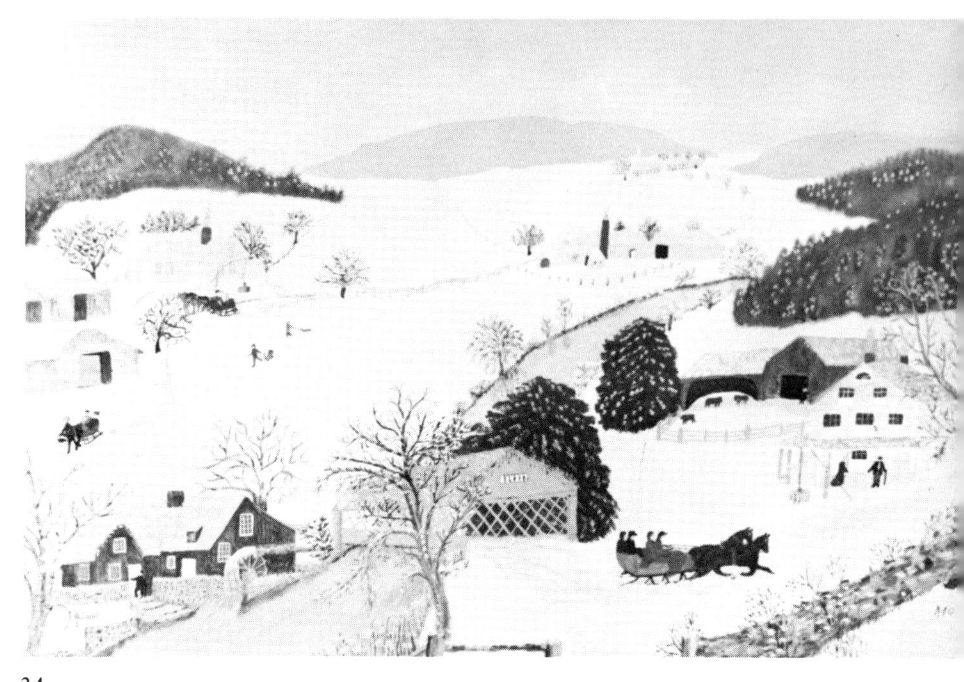

34

OVER THE RIVER TO GRANDMA'S HOUSE
1944

This was my Grandmother King's old house, and when Thanksgiving came we were all expected home to dinner. There were many young people like ourselves, and we would have a grand time in playing. Sports of all kinds, as we were of different ages, some old some young.

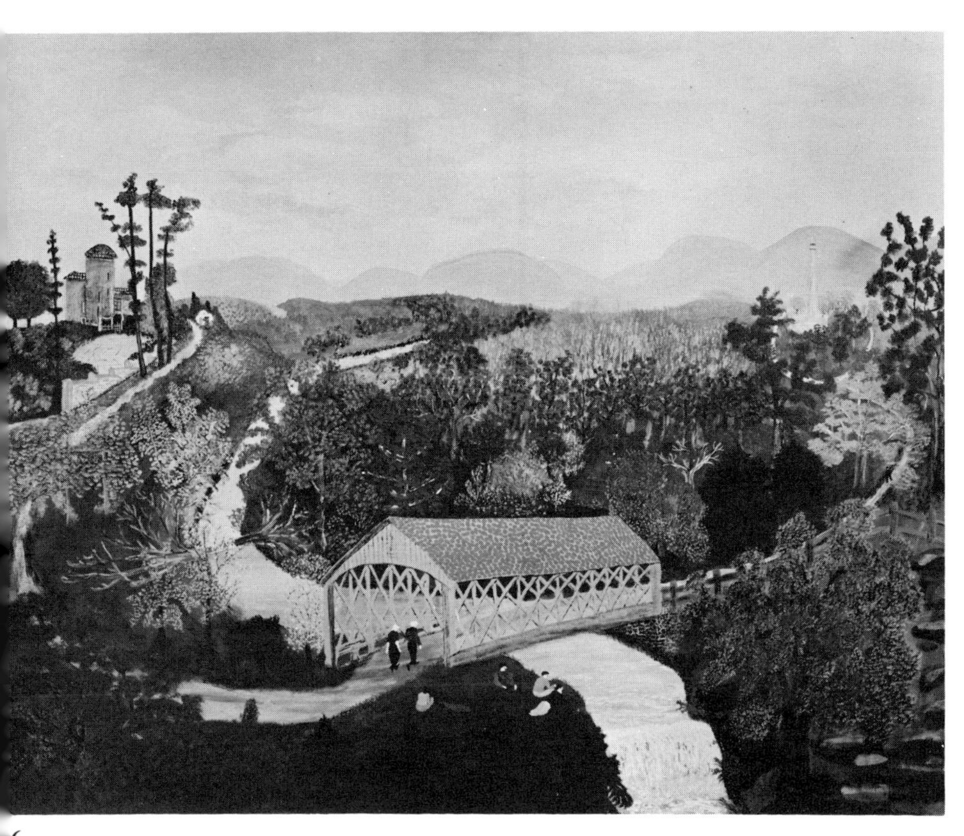

IN THE PARK
1944

Meaning nearer God's intentions, nearer to nature,
where in some respects, we are free,
where there is beauty and tranquillity,
where we sometimes long to be, quiet and
undisturbed, free from the hubbub of life.

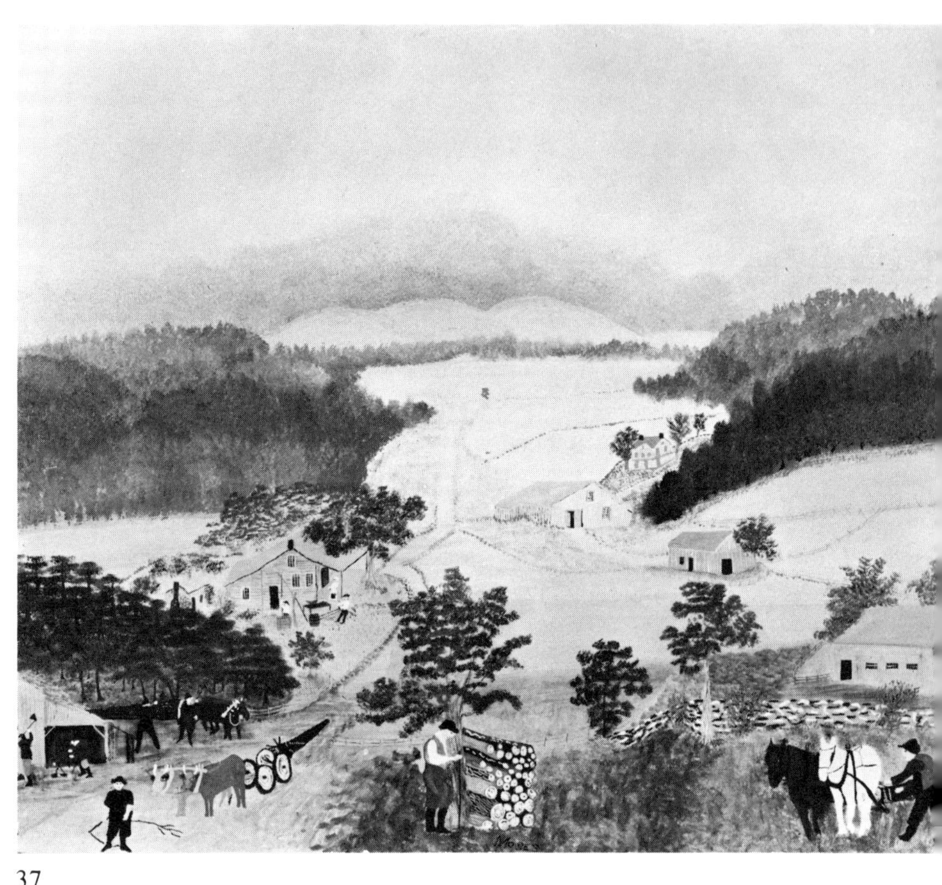

37

FIRST WAGON ON CAMBRIDGE PIKE
1944

My father's other grandfather was Archibald Robertson, born in Scotland in 1748, came to this country about 1770, coming to the Cambridge Valley. He was a wagon maker by trade. He built the first wagon that ever ran over the Cambridge Pike, building it with an axe and saw.

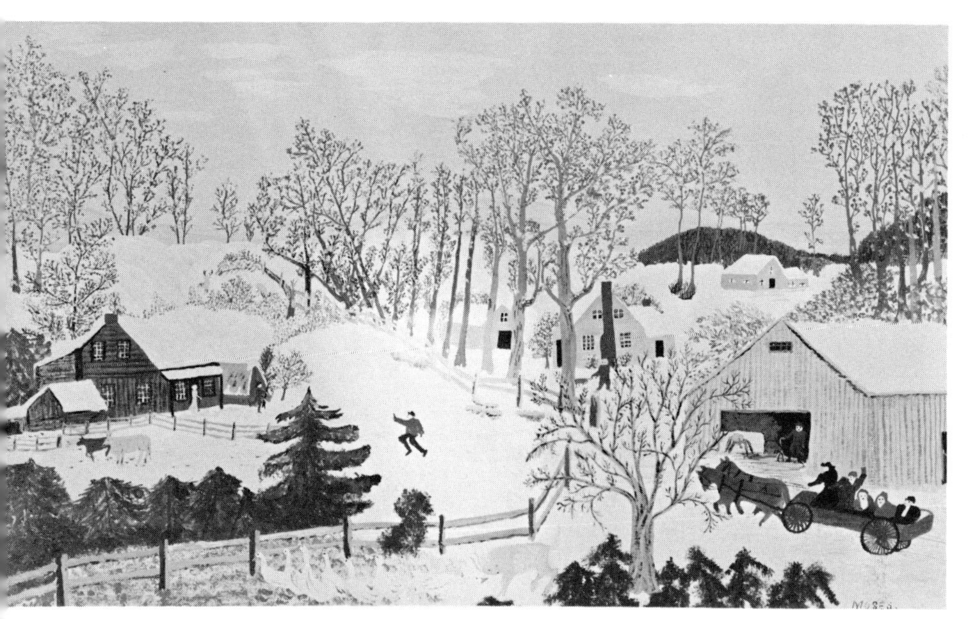

38

EARLY SPRINGTIME ON THE FARM
1945

In the springtime of life there is a plenty to do. Oh, those damp snowy days, early in spring, when we loved to go to the woods, and look for the first bloom of the trailing arbutus, which sometimes blooms beneath the snow, or gather the pussy willows.

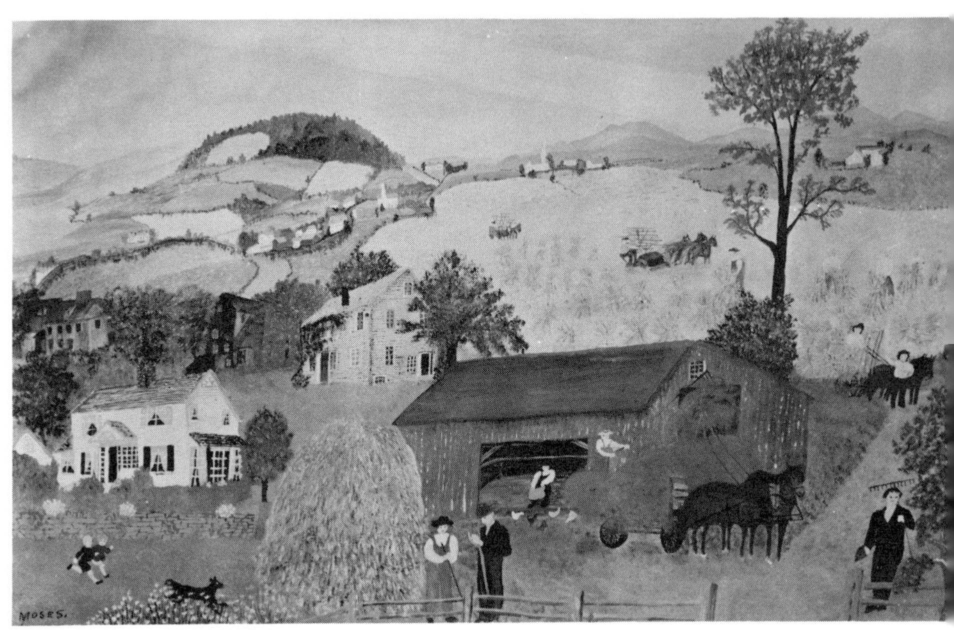

39

IN HARVEST TIME
1945

Haying time on the farm, when they gather the grain, fruit and berries of all description, and the little folks gather the eggs. When the church picnic comes, and the children can have all the cake and lemonade they want, water melon and peanuts, what a wonderful treat!

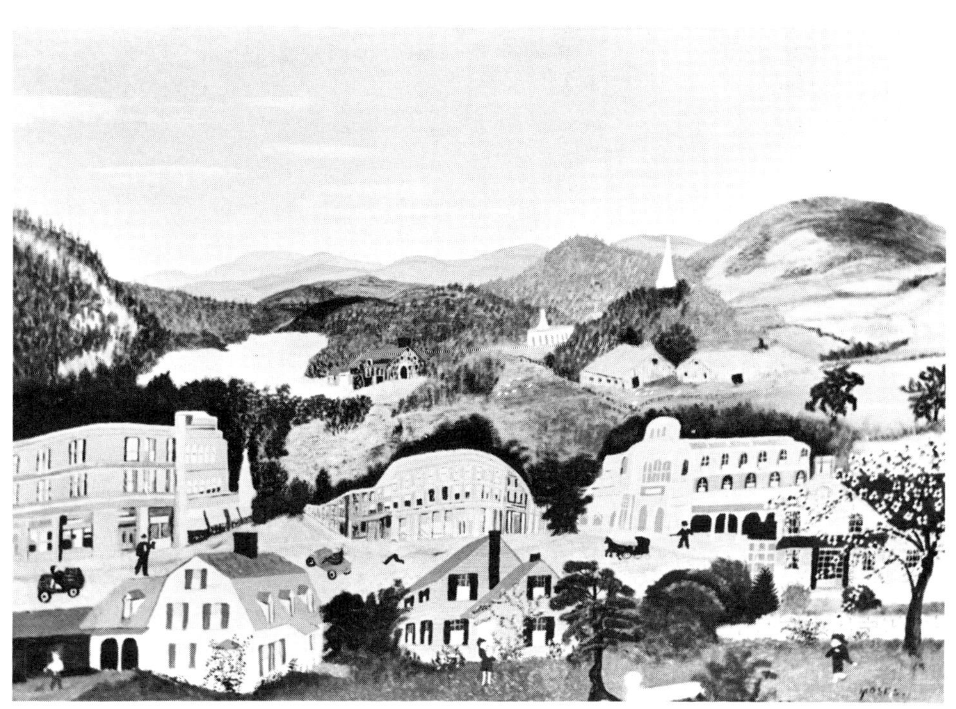

40

BENNINGTON
1945

Grandma Moses' daughter Anna was married to Walter Moses and lived in Bennington. There the artist visited her often. After the untimely death of Anna, Mrs. Moses lived in Bennington for two years to take care of her two grandchildren Zoan and Frances.

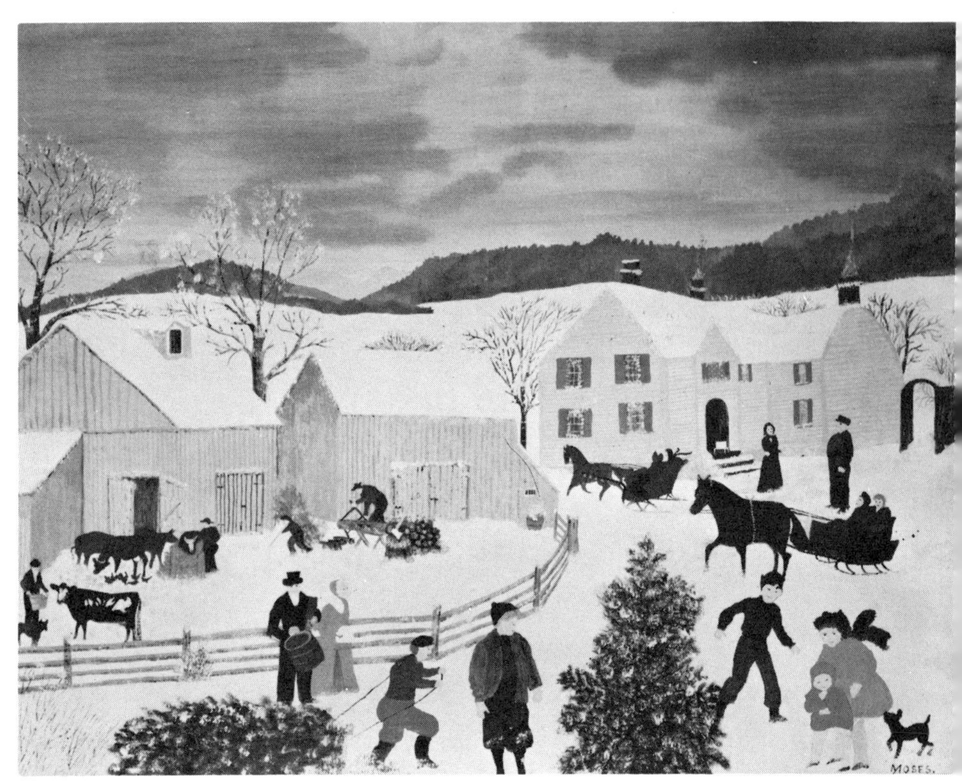

41

HERE COMES AUNT JUDITH
(BRINGING IN THE CHRISTMAS TREE)
1946

Oh with what joy and pleasure as we get together,
to go for the Christmas tree.
What aircastles we build as we slide down the hill.
Oh who can rebuild what we see on that Christmas tree.

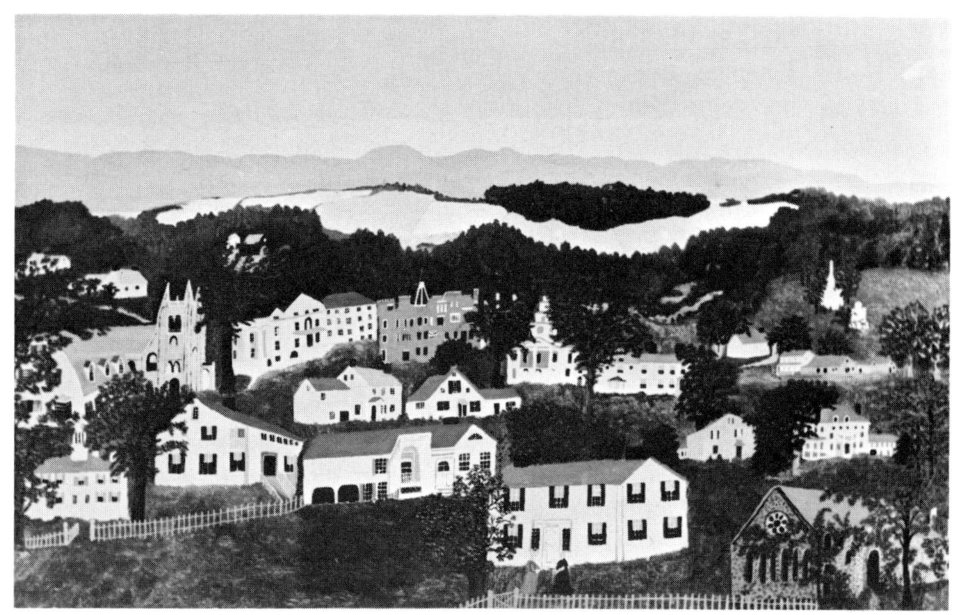

45

WILLIAMSTOWN
1947

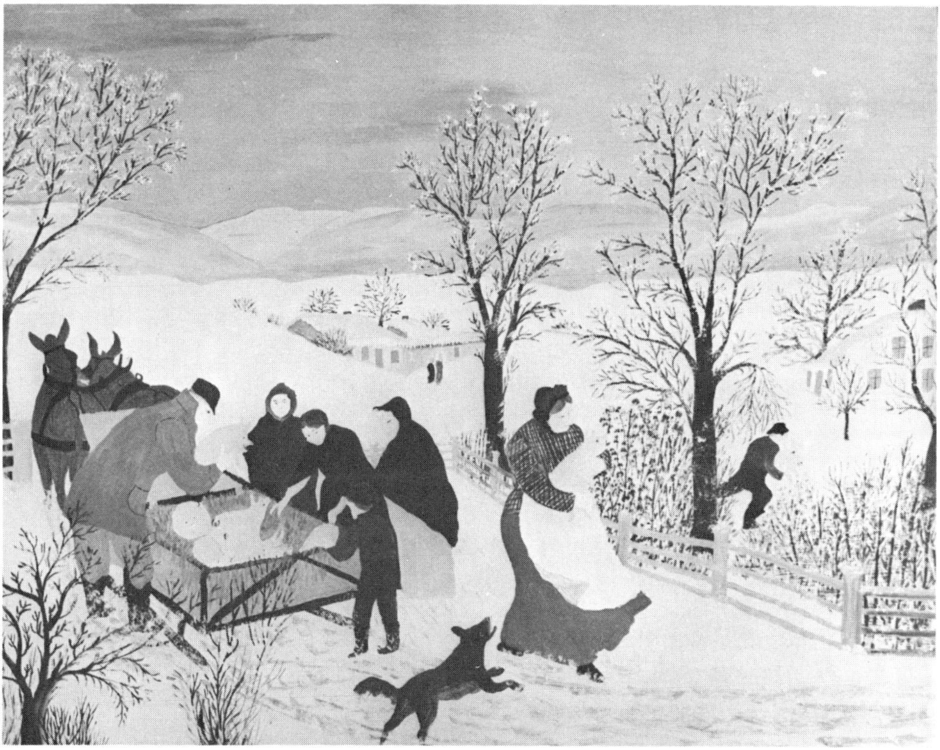

46

TOM TOM PIPER'S SON
1947

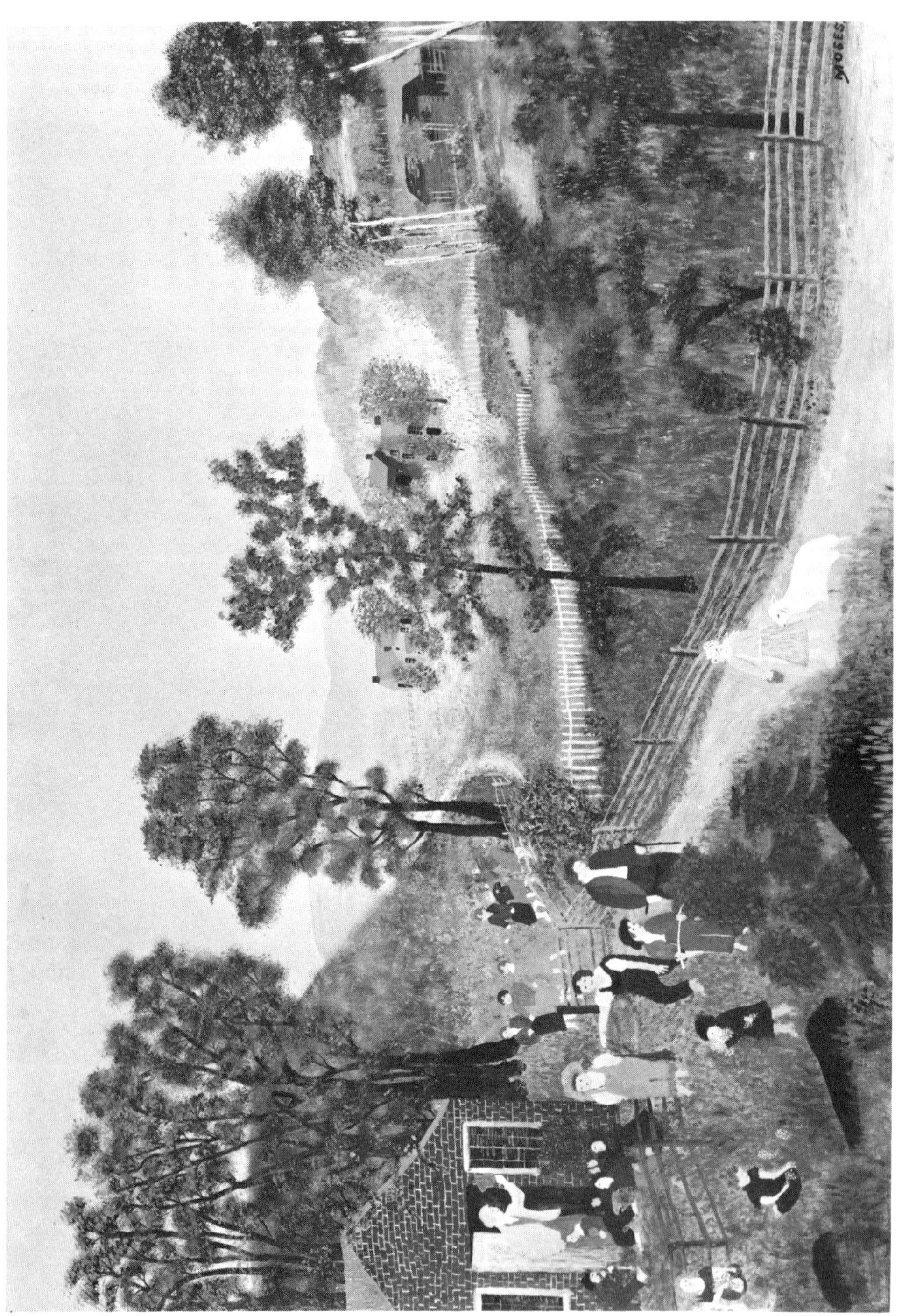
MOSES

MARY AND LITTLE LAMB
1947

Mary had a little lamb,
Its fleece was white as snow,
And everywhere that Mary went
The lamb was sure to go:
It followed her to school one day,—
That was against the rule;
It made the children laugh and play
To see a lamb at school.

And so the teacher turned him out,
But still he lingered near,
And waited patiently about,
Till Mary did appear;
And then he ran to her and laid
His head upon her arm—
As if he said—"I'm not afraid,
You'll keep me from all harm."

"What makes the lamb love Mary so?"
The little children cry,—
"Oh! Mary loves the lamb, you know,"
The teacher did reply;
"And you each gentle animal
In confidence may bind,
And make them follow at your call,
If you are always kind."

Sarah Hale.

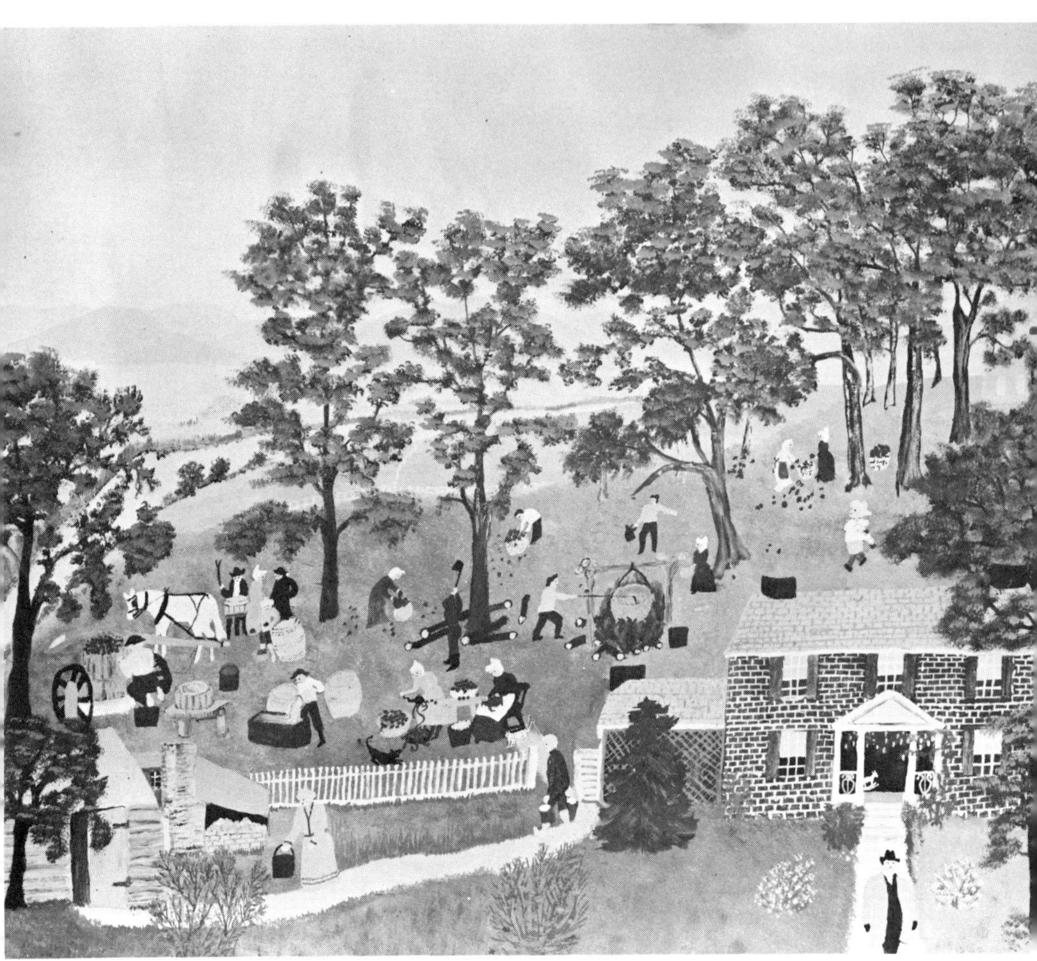

44

APPLE BUTTER MAKING
1947

Late Summer was the time for apple butter making. The apple butter was considered a necessity. Early in the season we would make cherry butter, we would make it up by the gallon, those stone gallon jars—I have got one left.

To make apple butter, you take two barrels of sweet cider (you grind apples and make sweet cider first), then you put them on in a big brass kettle over a fire out in the orchard and start it to boiling. You want three barrels of quartered apples, or snits, as they called them, with cores taken out, and then you commence to feed those in, and stirring and keeping that stirrer going. The stirrer was a very long stick which would rest on the kettle, with a smaller stick that was held in by a peg going to the bottom of the kettle. Women folks would keep that going, feeding in all the apples till evening. Then the young folks would come in to start stirring. They'd have a regular frolic all night out in the orchard. If they'd get this started early enough in the morning, they'd have to stir till about midnight, when it would get thick enough. Then you pour in—if you want it sweet and pleasant—maybe 20 pounds of sugar, and then you put in either cinnamon or clove oil, whatever you like best, and keep tasting it till you have got the right sourness or sweetness and the right flavor. About that time you bring out your jars, around the fire that has gone down, not too hot. We would make about 40 gallons at a time. It was very much like a jelly Conserve.

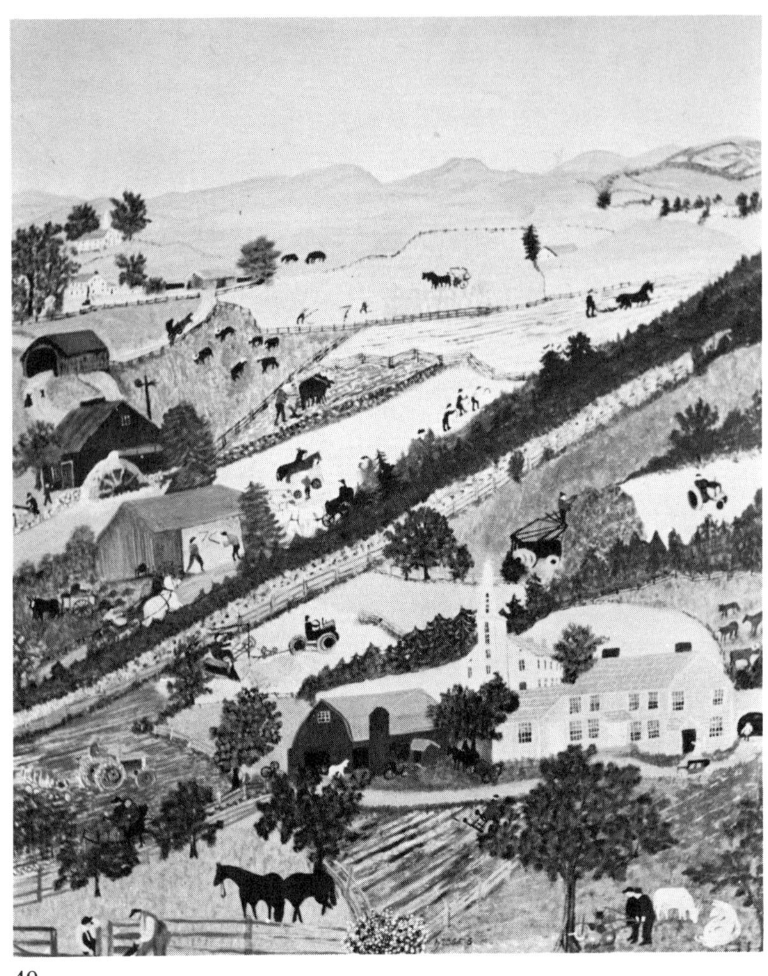

49

YEAR 1860—YEAR 1940
1948

In this picture Grandma Moses wanted to show the agricultural methods of the 19th century as contrasted with modern techniques. Note, especially, the stone fence marking the boundary of the upper, early part next to the wooden fence where the lower, contemporary section begins.

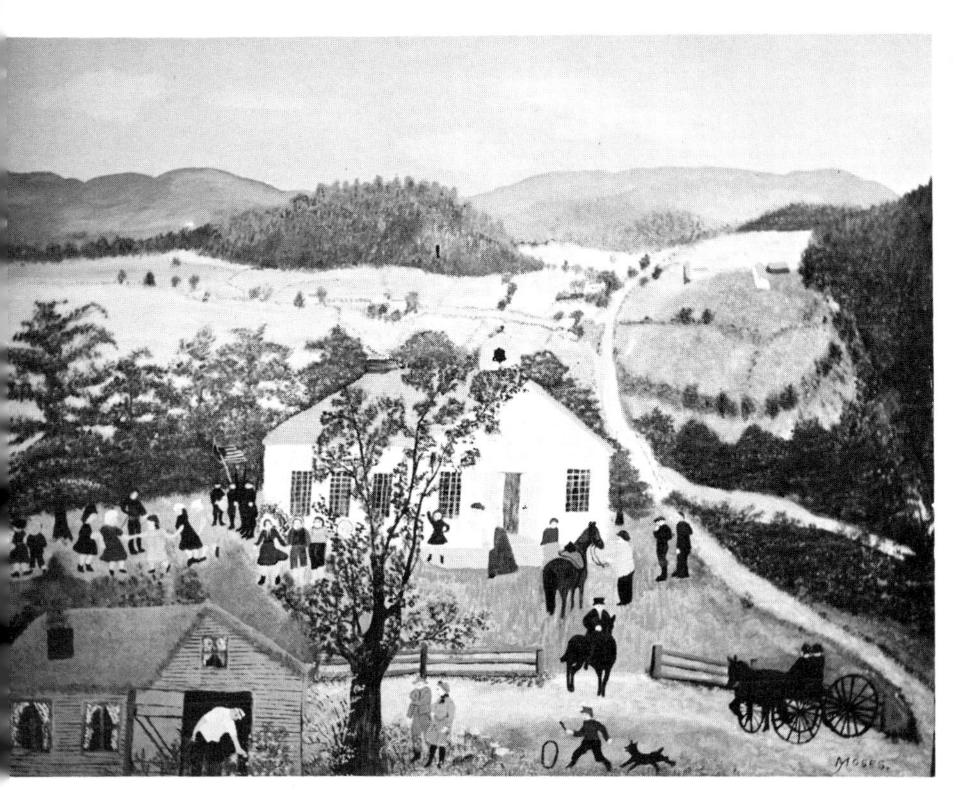

THE SCHOOL HOUSE
1949

Schooling was in those days in the country three months in summer, three in winter; little girls did not go to school much in the winter, owing to the cold, and not warm enough clothing, therefore my school days were limited, but I was kept busy helping at home and the neighbors.

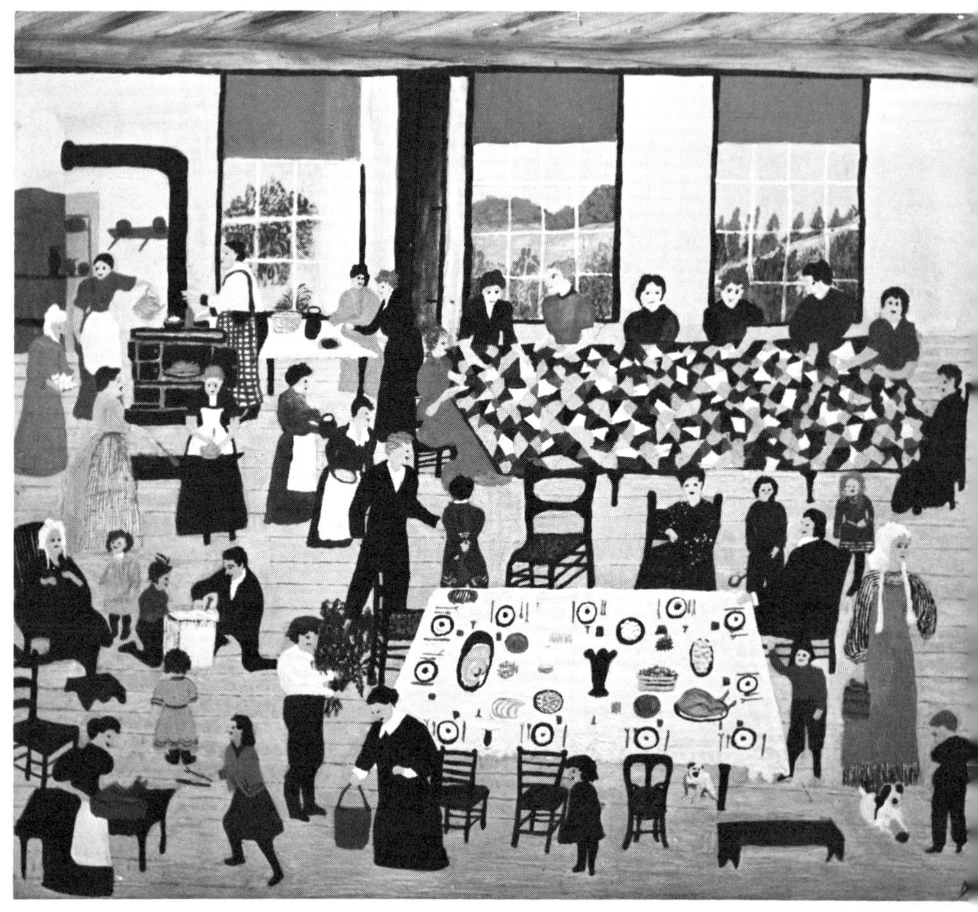
50

THE QUILTING BEE
1950

Back in Revolutionary War times quilting bees were a necessity as well as thing of art. The women took great pride in their needle work. Every well regulated house had one room set aside which was called the quilting room; the quilting frames were set up on the backs of chairs or stands.

The women of the neighborhood would gather to sew, sometimes at night, but candle light was very poor for fine stitches, which the women of those days prided themselves in. Some of the designs were beautifully done, such as the Sunflower, Rising Sun and Friendship, where each one wrote her name in the center of the block.

There are a few of those old quilts scattered through the country, highly cherished by their owners.

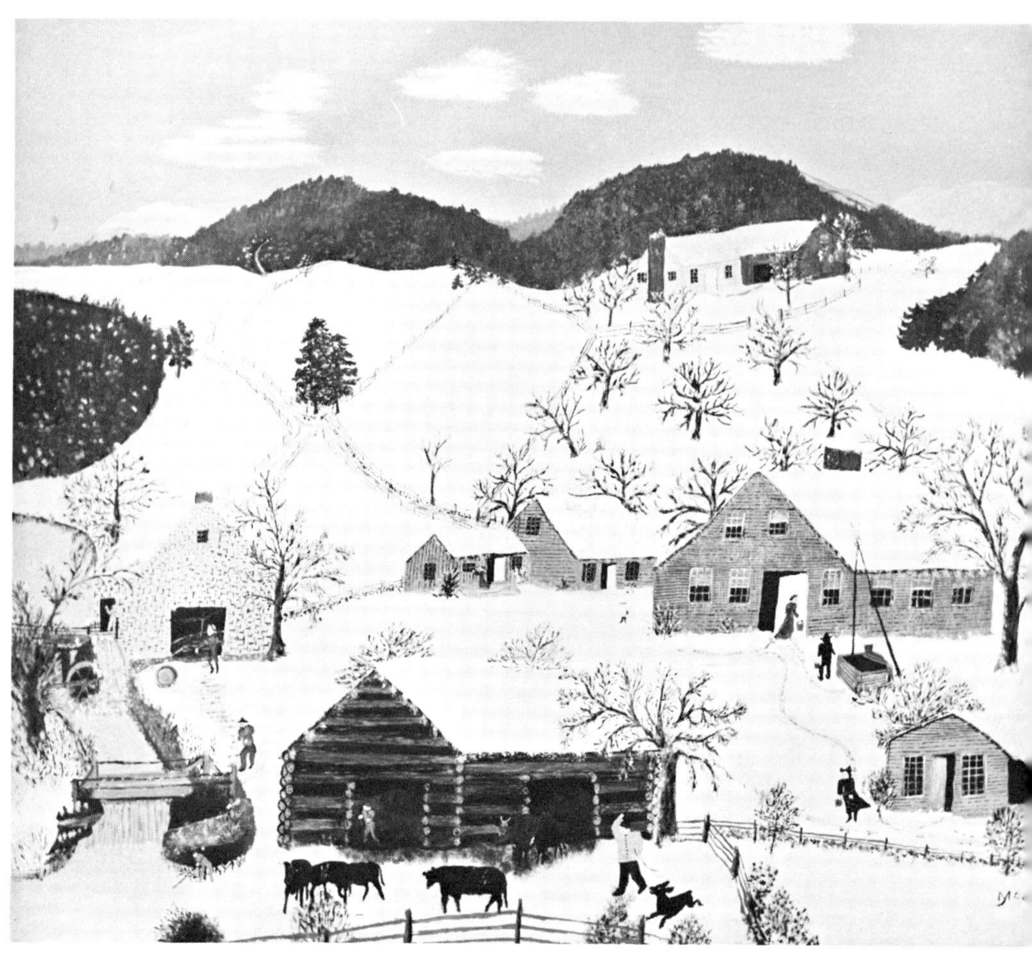

51

THE OLD OAKEN BUCKET IN WINTER
1950

I have been asked why I painted the Old Oaken Bucket. I have painted a good many of them, and I wish now that I had sent the history with them. It would have been a monument to that poor forgotten boy Paul Dennis. When I was 17, Mrs. David Burch, an old lady, and I were getting a drink of water at a well and she said: "Do you know what a well you are drinking from?" No, I did not know. Then she told me that was the well of the Old Oaken Bucket and went on telling me the history: "Situated in the town of Cambridge, Washington Co., N.Y., back in the year of 1760, this was the childhood home of Paul Dennis. He liked one of the neighbor's daughters and her father thought Paul not good enough for her, and that made trouble. So Paul left the country and went off to be a sailor. And he was quite young and very homesick. It was then he wrote those verses of the Old Oaken Bucket. When returning to Boston after three years he gave the verses to Woodworth who set them to music, and therefore claimed them as his composing."

In the winter of 1940 I had the grippe, and they kept me in bed, and I planned mischief then. When I was lying there, I thought I was going to paint the story of the "Old Oaken Bucket," because I knew how it originated. I painted it when I got up, that was the first one I tried, but later I painted it again and could remember more of the details.

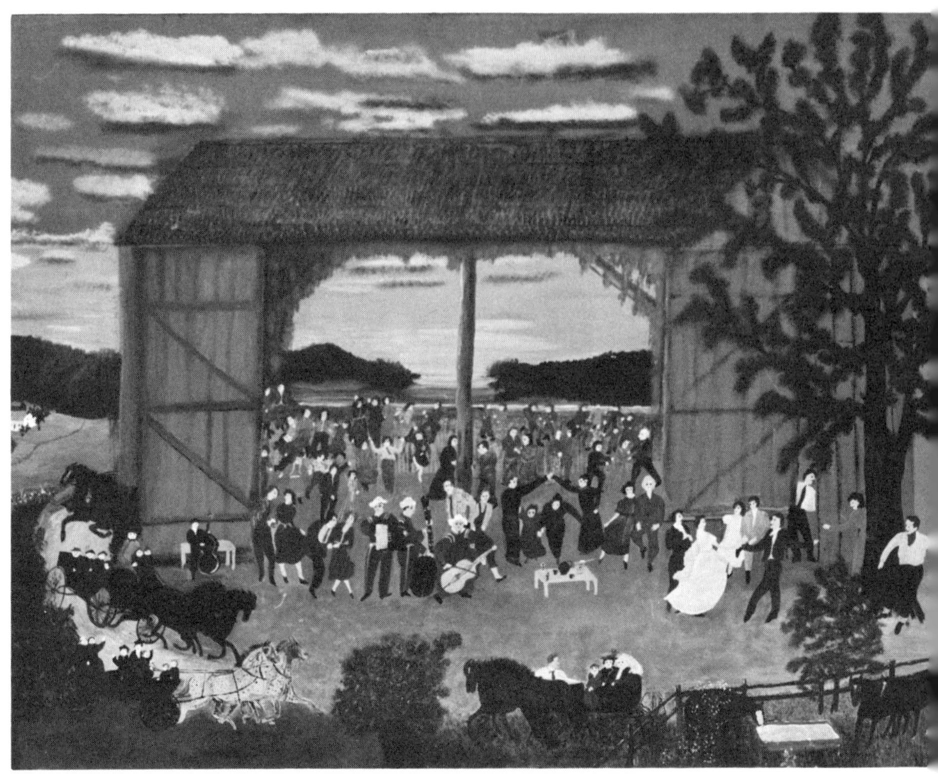

55

THE BARN DANCE
1950

I was never friendly with any boy except my husband. Oh, we'd go to the country dances, but the next day I would feel so mean and dirty from dancing with this one and that one. They were just dances to entertain and spend the evening, somebody would play the harmonica, anything for fun, it whiled away the time.

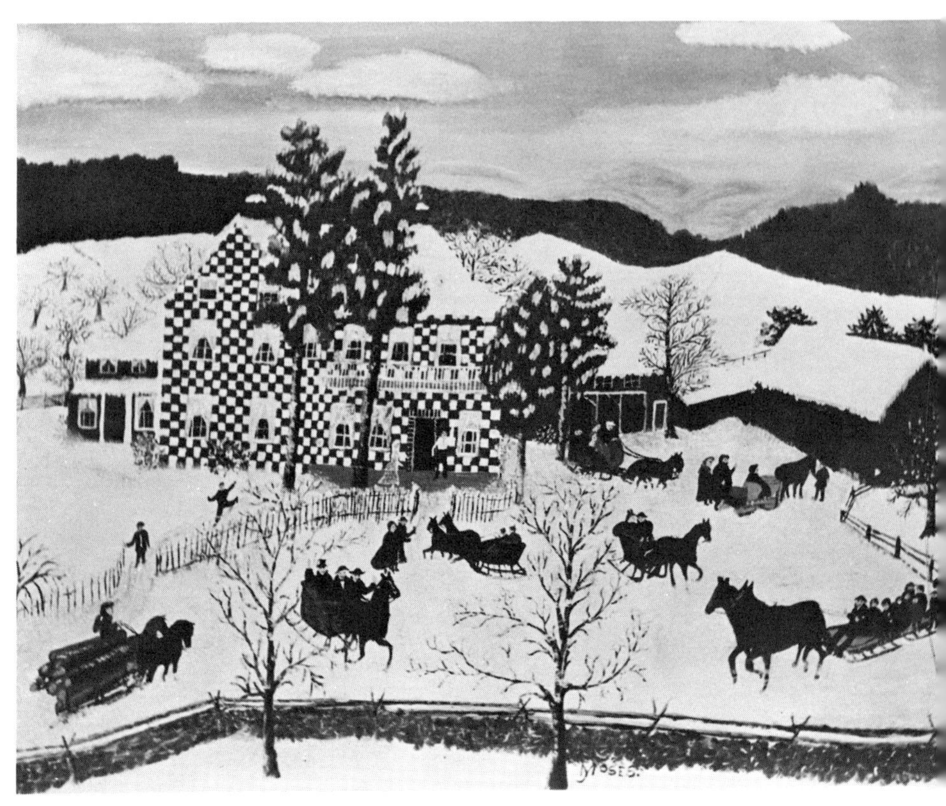

52

THE OLD CHECKERED HOUSE
1950

The Checkered House is old. It was the Headquarters of General Baum in the Revolutionary War, and afterwards he used it as a hospital, then it was a stopping place for the stage, where they changed horses every two miles. Oh we travelled fast *in those days.*

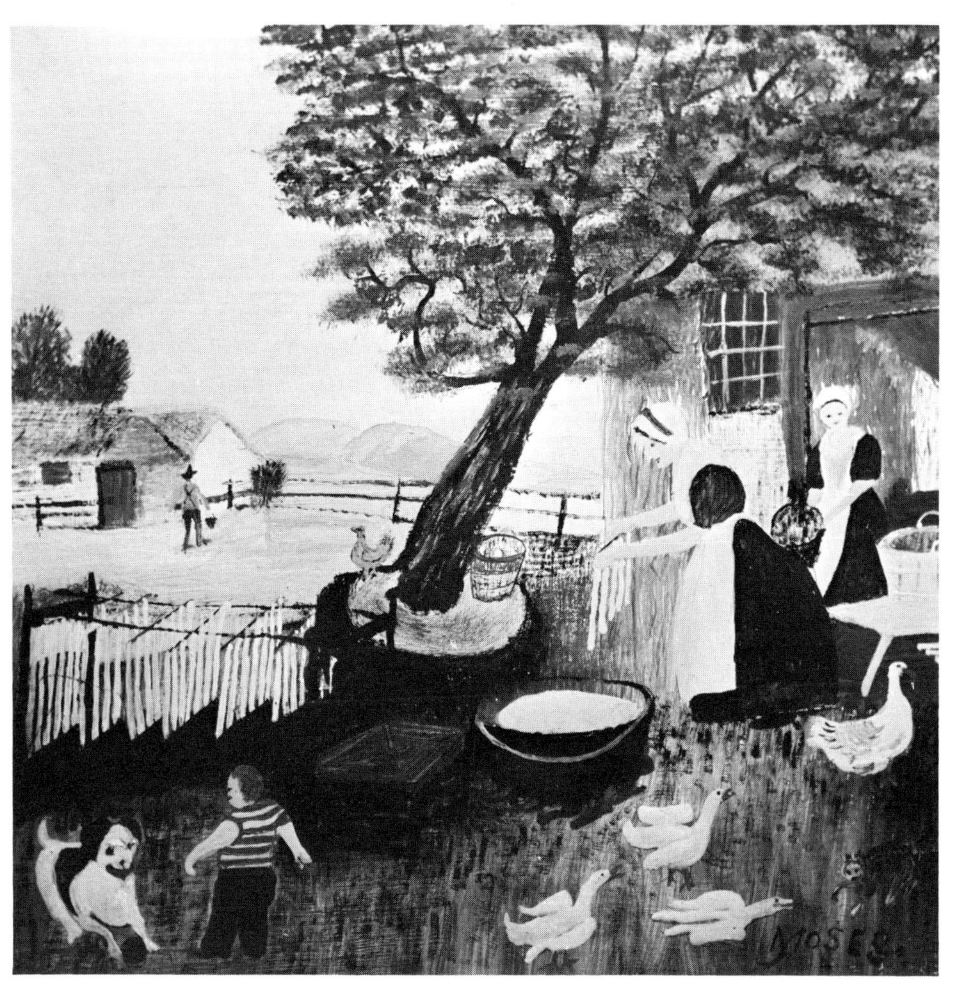

56

CANDLE DIP DAY
1950

The minute it come around cool weather, we commence to make candles for the following year. We thread candle molds with candle wicking and then melt up some of the tallow and pour it from the top into the candle mold, so it runs down into the mold. Then we set it outdoors for it to harden. The children and the hired girl and the lady of the house, everybody had a chance in it, depending on who was the most idle—the same as we washed dishes. It was tiresome for me, I'd rather be outdoors playing, but it was a necessary job.

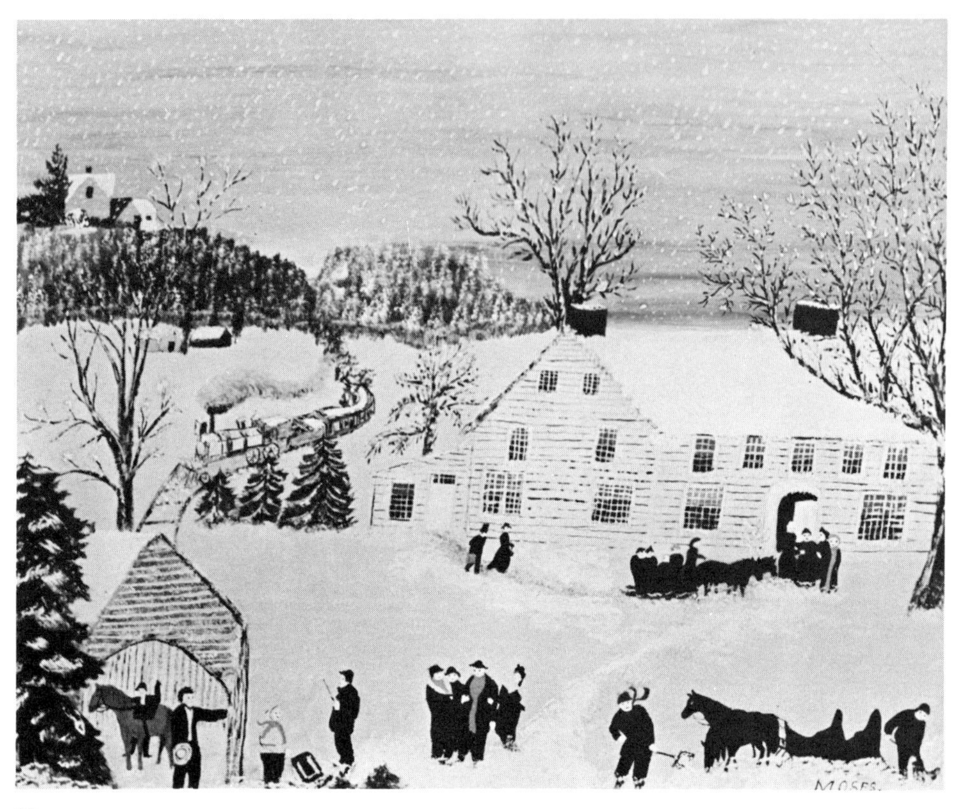

61

THE DEPARTURE
1951

On September 20, 1887 Thomas Salmon Moses and Anna Mary Robertson decided to get married. Thomas, as I always called him, had said when he got ready to go for himself, he was a'going to a warmer climate, so we decided to go South.

On the morning of the 9th of November I bid mother and father goodbye for the time, not knowing when I would see them again. We had to hurry over to take the six o'clock train to New York City. As luck would have it, it was an excursion train, and all the neighbors were on it. They'd all come and congratulate us, and they scolded him for taking away the best girl in the country.

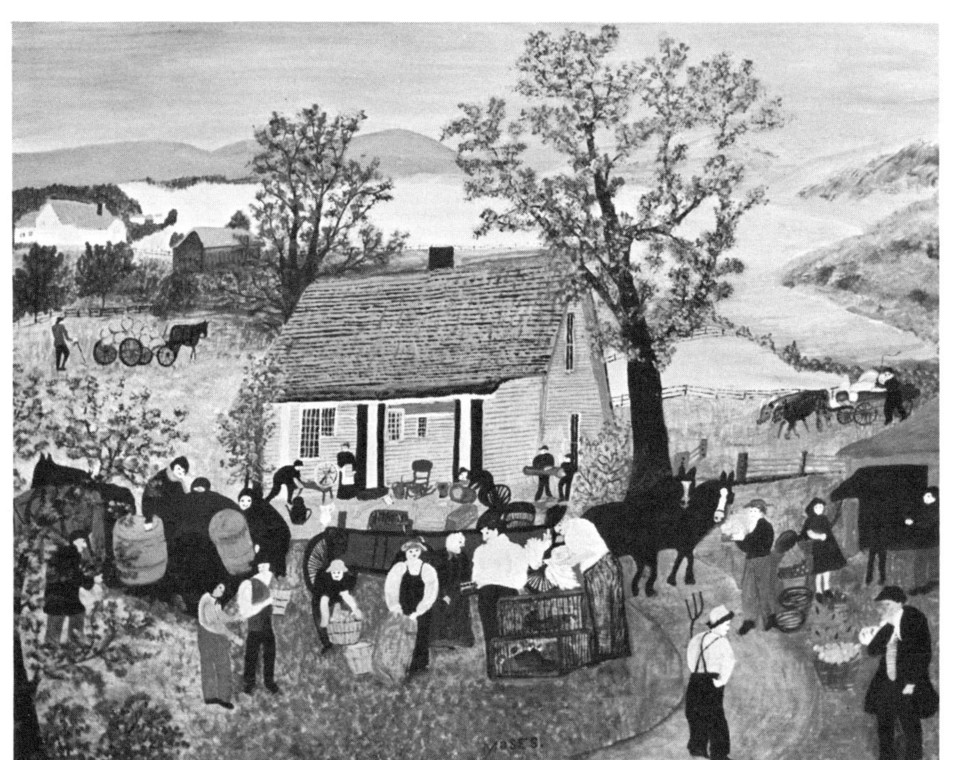

59

MOVING DAY
1951

In 1905 we commenced to prepare on moving back. We chartered a railroad car, and we brought the stuff we had—a piano and beds and necessary things up here that way. We could bring a lot of produce—a cow, hens, and stock. In one corner was the cow tied up with the feed. But at one place, where they were switching off, the jolt was so strong, it knocked the cow off her feet, and tipped the stove. The price of the car was $60. I think that was a pretty cheap trip.

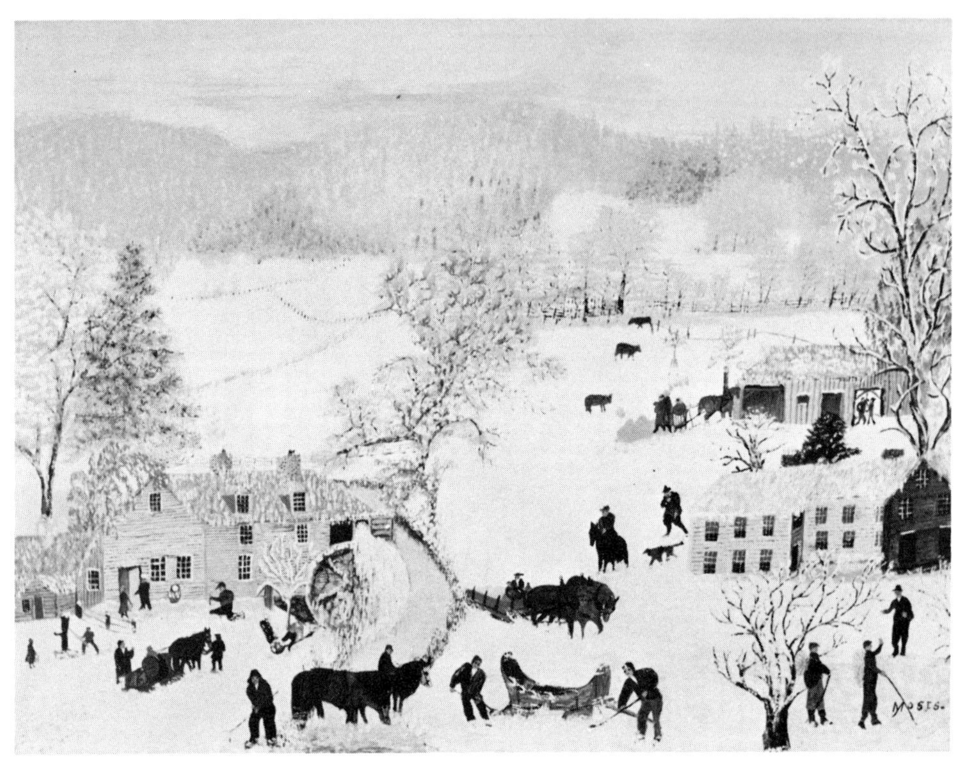

63

A FROSTY DAY
1951

And then wintertime! When zero stands at 25 or 30, when we cannot deny the pleasure of skating till we have bumped heads and bleedy noses, and the ice is like glass.

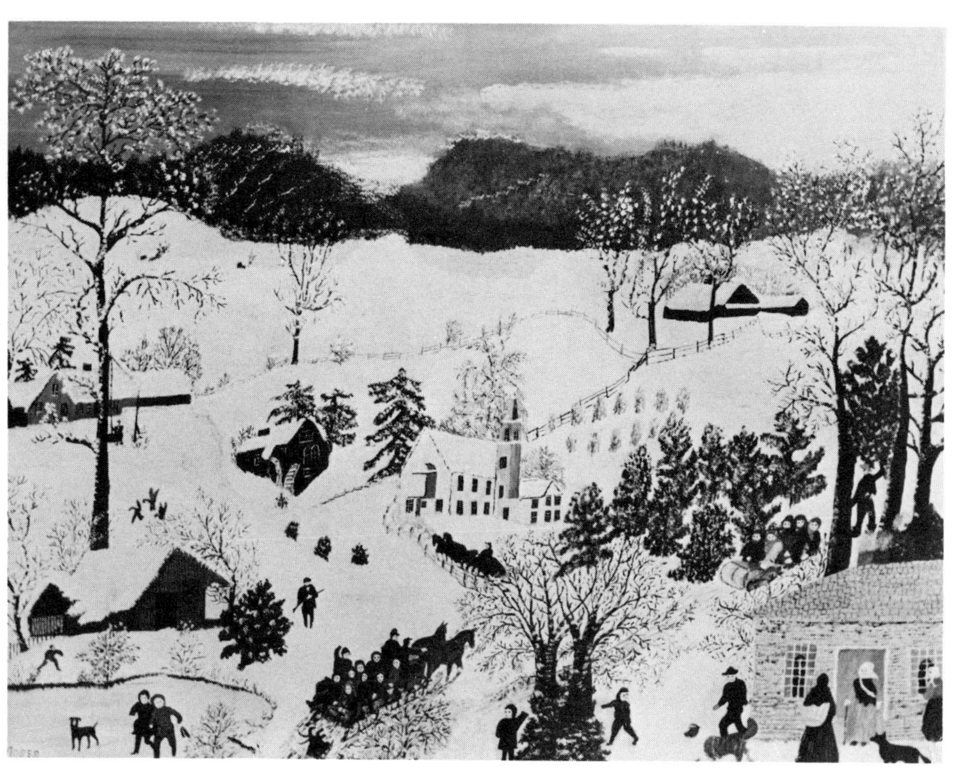

62

IT SNOWS, OH IT SNOWS
1951

. . . Then the sun came out and melted the snow on top, and then it froze so hard, it would almost hold up a horse. It was so cold, my brothers could not go to school, and we played on the crust on the snow. Lester had a sleigh with cast iron runners, Horace had an old wash bench, upside down, but very safe, Arthur a dust pan, and I an old scoop shovel. Oh, what fun! We would play out for hours, and the thermometer at 25 below zero.

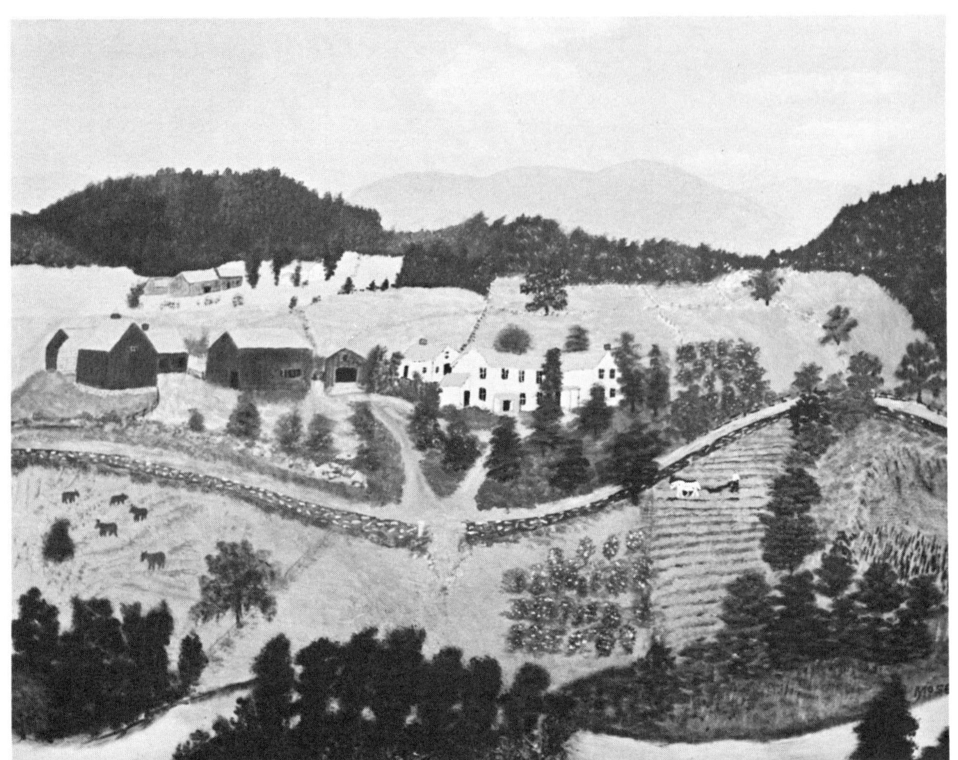

64

MOSES
1953

Well time passed on, on a farm the days are nearly all the same, nothing changes but the seasons.

Life was a sort of routine. Monday washday, Tuesday ironing and mending, Wednesday baking and cleaning, Thursday sewing, Friday sewing and odd jobs, such as working in the garden or with flowers. And thus it was from year to year.

It was a rollicksome, happy house, and their father would join in with the children, he was really one of them.

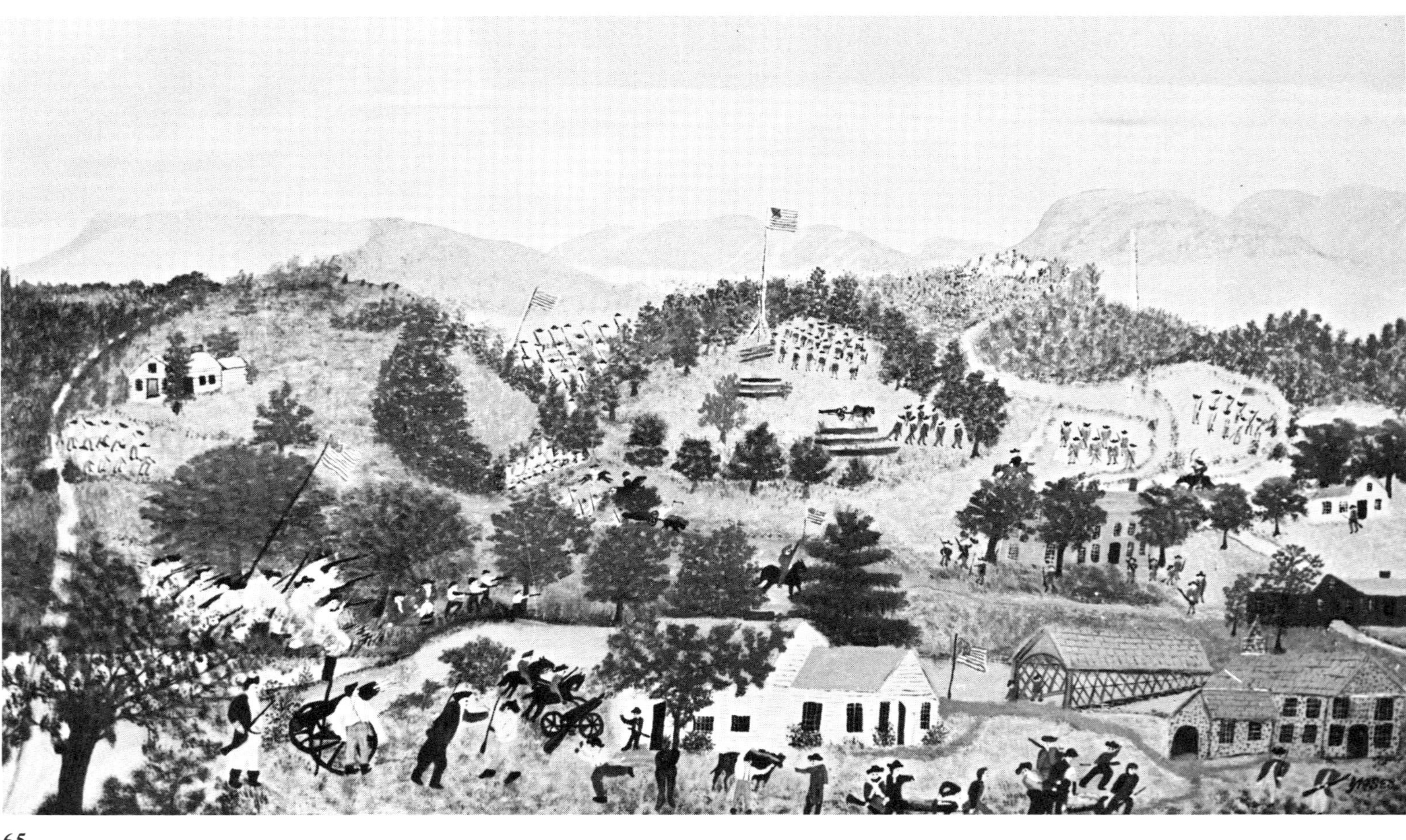

THE BATTLE OF BENNINGTON
1953

In 1953 the National Society of Daughters of the American Revolution asked Grandma Moses to paint a picture of historical content to be hung in the National Society's Museum in Washington, D. C. Always interested in the American Revolution, Grandma Moses decided to depict the Battle of Bennington in Battlefield Park. Before commencing her work, she looked up many historical details in a variety of reference books. When the painting, which is here displayed, was finished, Grandma's family and friends remarked that the monument in the background, surely, had not been erected at the time of the battle. Not satisfied with this first version, Grandma Moses painted another one, this time omitting the monument. That picture is now in the possession of the D.A.R.

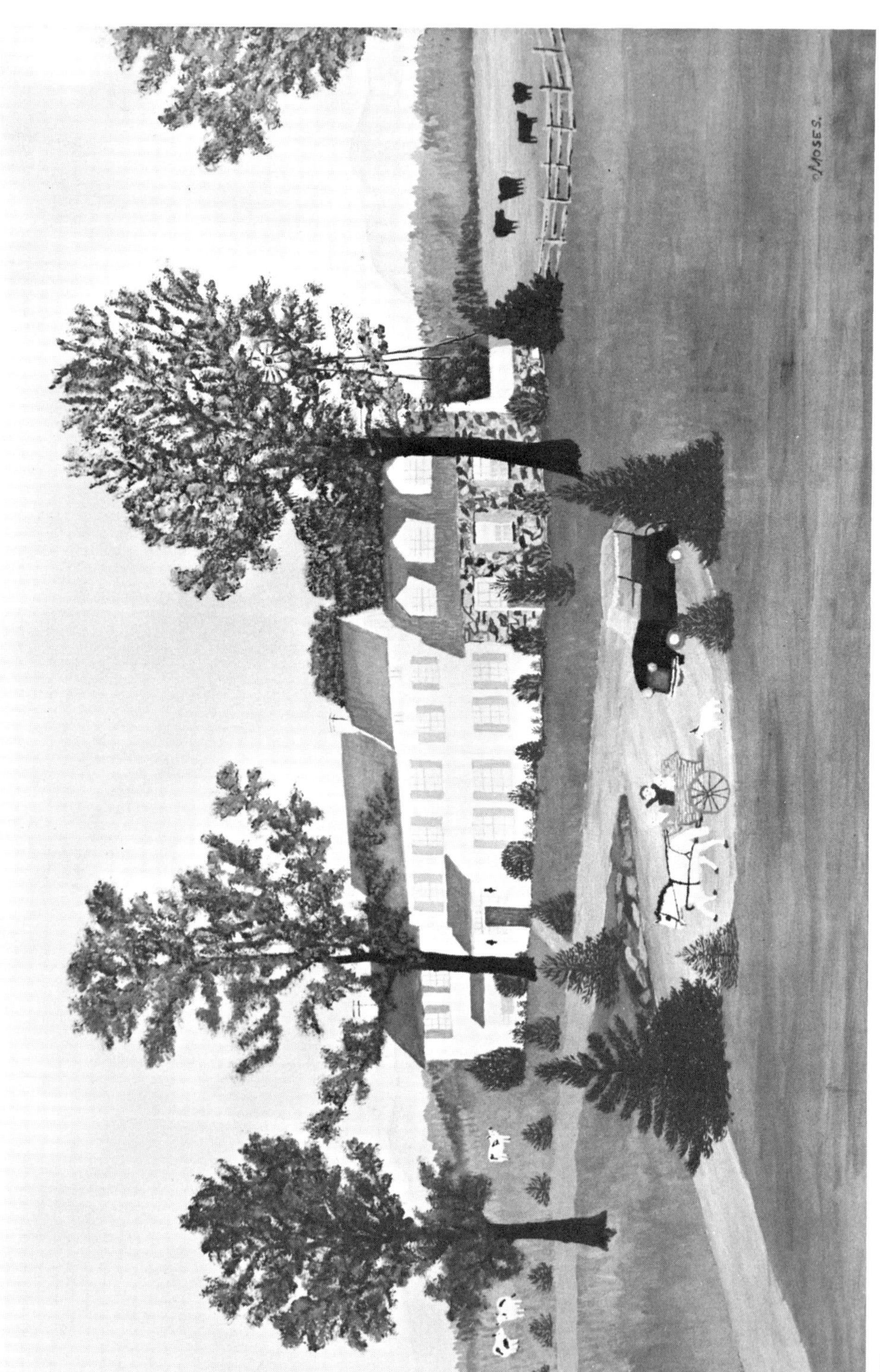
MOSES.

EISENHOWER HOME
1956

In December of 1955 Grandma Moses received an urgent phone call from the White House. Mr. Harold Stassen asked her to paint a picture of the Eisenhower farm in Gettysburg, Pa., to be given to the President by the Cabinet on the third anniversary of his Inauguration, the following month.

Although Grandma Moses had been painting her "memories and imagination" most of the time, she promised to try to compose a picture from photographs which the White House sent her. She became so engrossed with the subject, that she did not one but two different paintings. Both contain elements from the photographs, and in addition, a few characteristics of her own.

The second version is exhibited here for the first time.

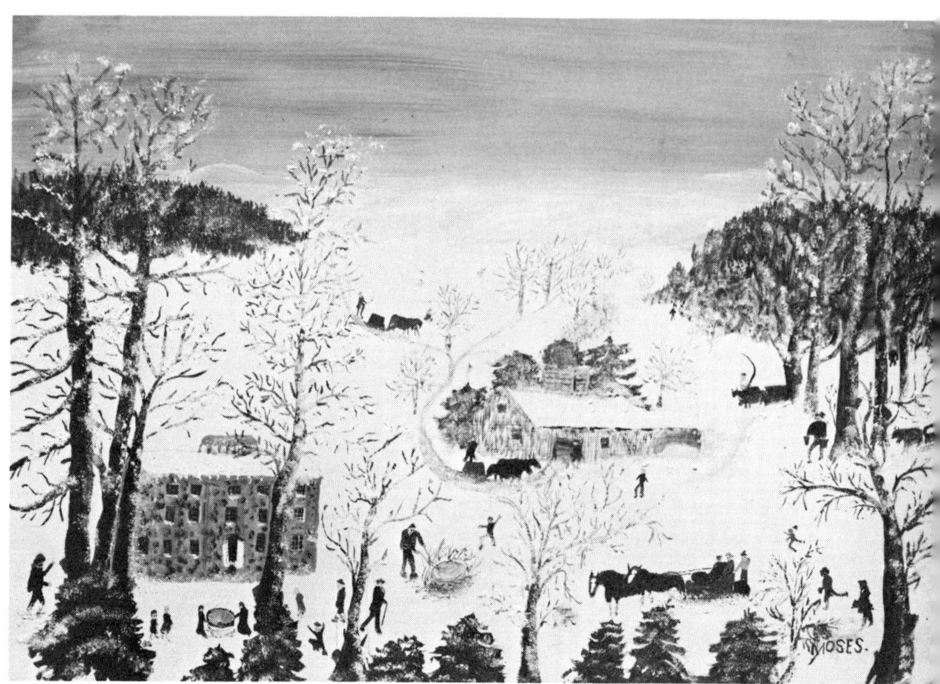

66

SUGARING
1955

In the summer of 1955 the late Edward R. Murrow, distinguished radio and television commentator, interviewed Grandma Moses at her home in Eagle Bridge for a "See It Now" program, subsequently telecast in the winter of that year. He wished to show the artist in her everyday surroundings and activities, and conversed with her while she was painting this picture.

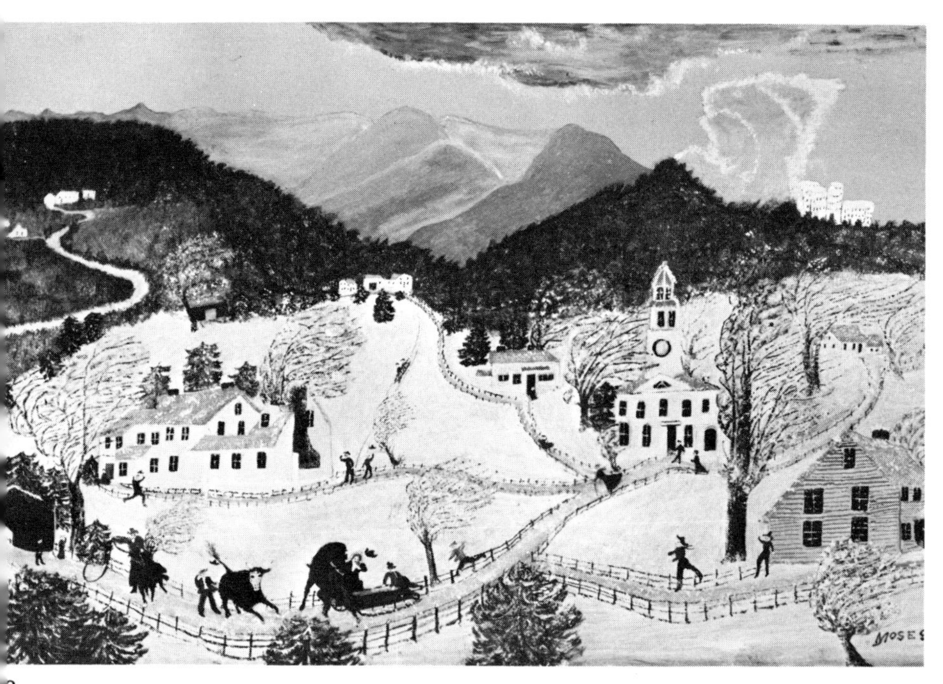

BLIZZARD
1956

It was a beautiful morning, but before noon it commenced to cloud up and got very cold, and that night it commenced to snow, and by morning there was two feet of snow on the ground.

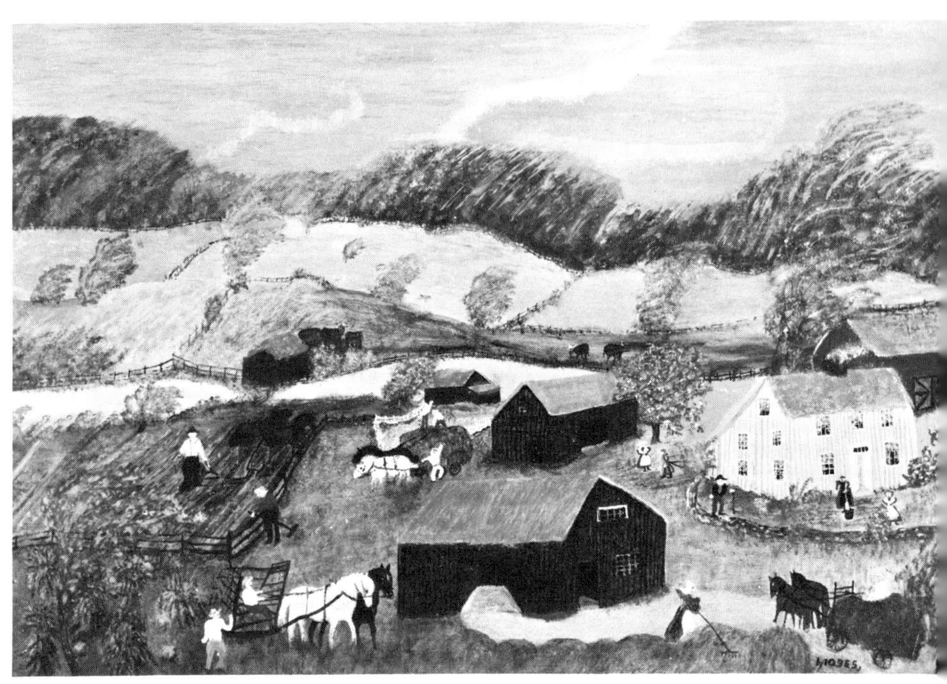

69

WIND STORM
1956

My first thunderstorm was in 1867. That had been a very hot summer in Washington County, New York. This Sunday it was very dry and warm, and the pond had nearly dried up, and mother said she would like to see it. And then here came the wind. It struck the tree tops and bent them to the ground, sweeping the yard clean. Then the rain came down in sheets. We thought the windows would break in, and mother told us to keep away from them.

That was the worst storm I ever saw in my childhood days.

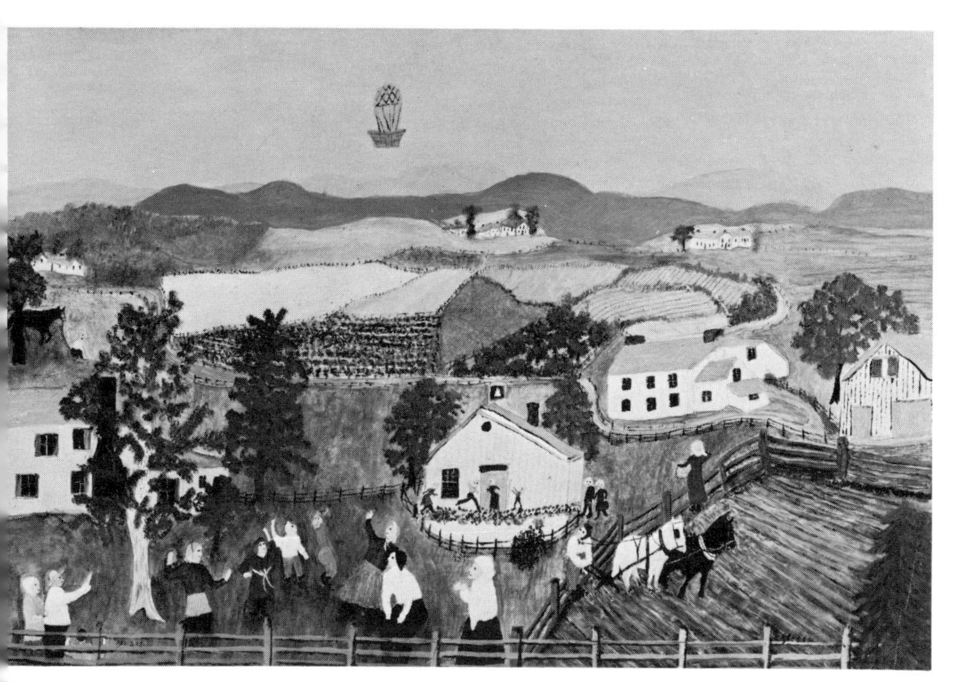

71

THE BALLOON
1957

It was the year of 1907. I remember seeing a balloon going over from Argyle to Cambridge, N. Y., there was a man, woman, and child in it. They landed in Cambridge. In 1911 there was lots of talb about the new invention, airplanes. Some time later I saw my first. And my first movie, I saw it in Syracuse in 1914. That was grand.

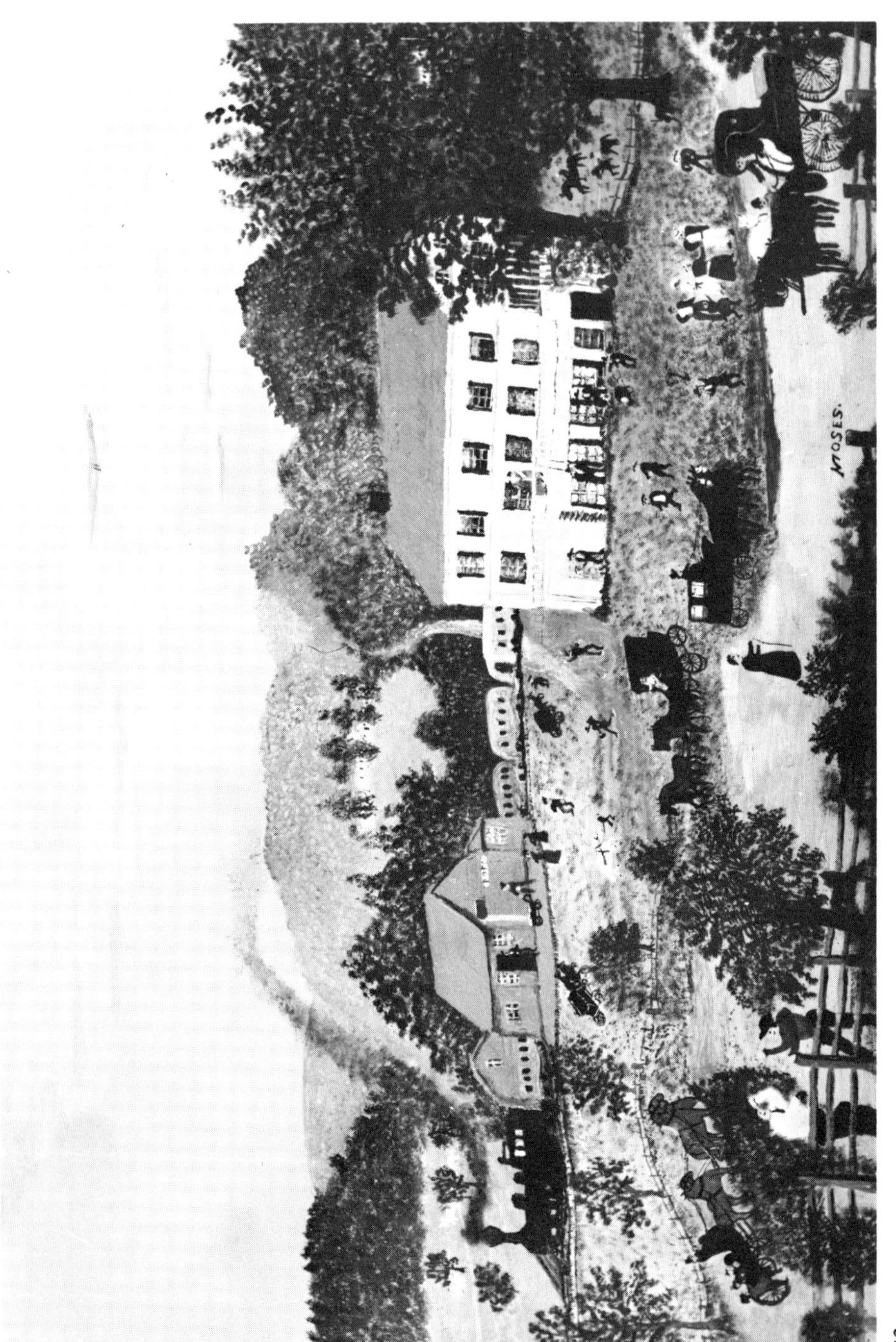
MOSES.

THE EAGLE BRIDGE HOTEL
1959

Eagle Bridge was a railroad center. The Eagle Bridge Hotel has been built three times, and burned every time. It had three stories with many bedrooms upstairs. They had great meals that were served at the hotel. Then they stopped doing that, since the days of the automobile. The local people came to the hotel for drinks. There were two hotels running at the same time, the Eagle Bridge Hotel and the Dalton House. People that came on the train would stop off here.

Eagle Bridge was in its prime in those days. You came to Eagle Bridge to get the results of the voting—that was a good excuse, always, they had couriers going from one place to the other to announce the election results. But they had another reason to come: to talk and to get a drink. The Eagle Bridge Hotel burned the last time around 1916.

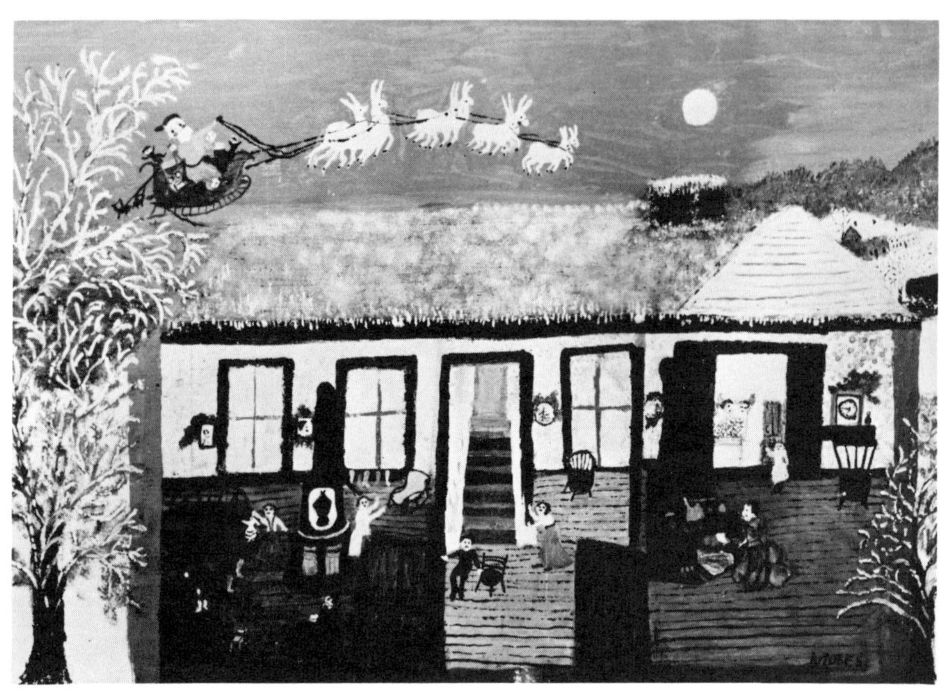

75

THE NIGHT BEFORE CHRISTMAS
1960

The first Christmas that I can remember I must have been four years old. I remember mother and father going to Greenwich to buy things, and leaving me and my two brothers at home with my aunt Lib, as we called her.

And when my mother came back, she told aunt Lib that Santa Claus had been up in Carpenter's store, and that she must go and see him. My brother Lester got very excited and wanted to clean out underneath the stove so that Santy could come down the stove pipe with his load of toys.

Three of several paintings done between April and June 1960, to illustrate the poem "The Night Before Christmas" by Clement C. Moore, Random House, New York, 1961.

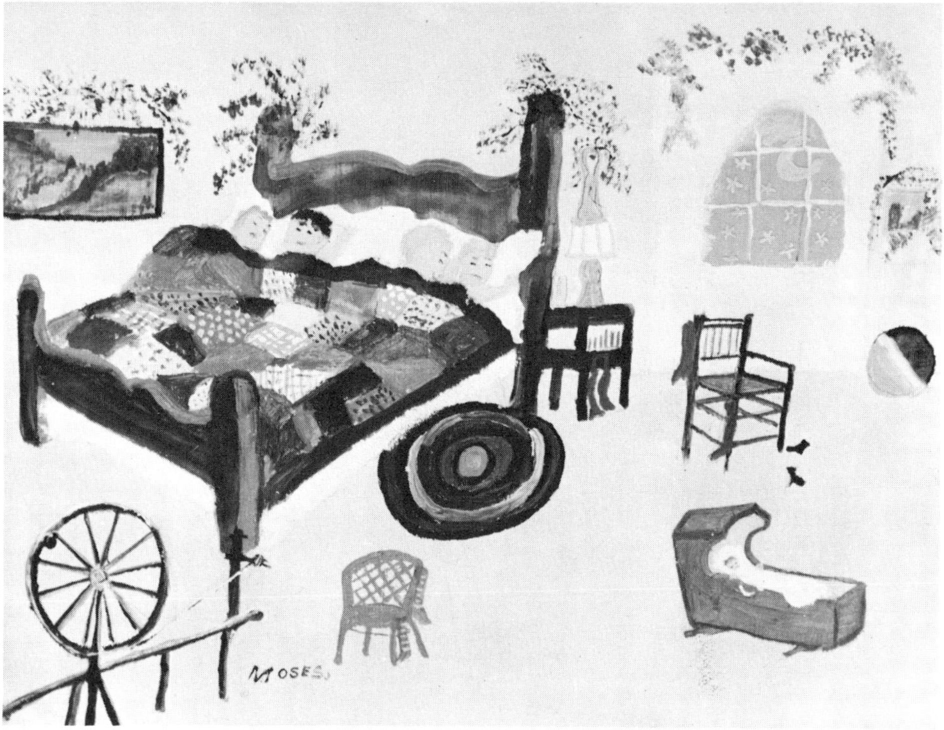

79

WAITING FOR SANTA CLAUS
1960

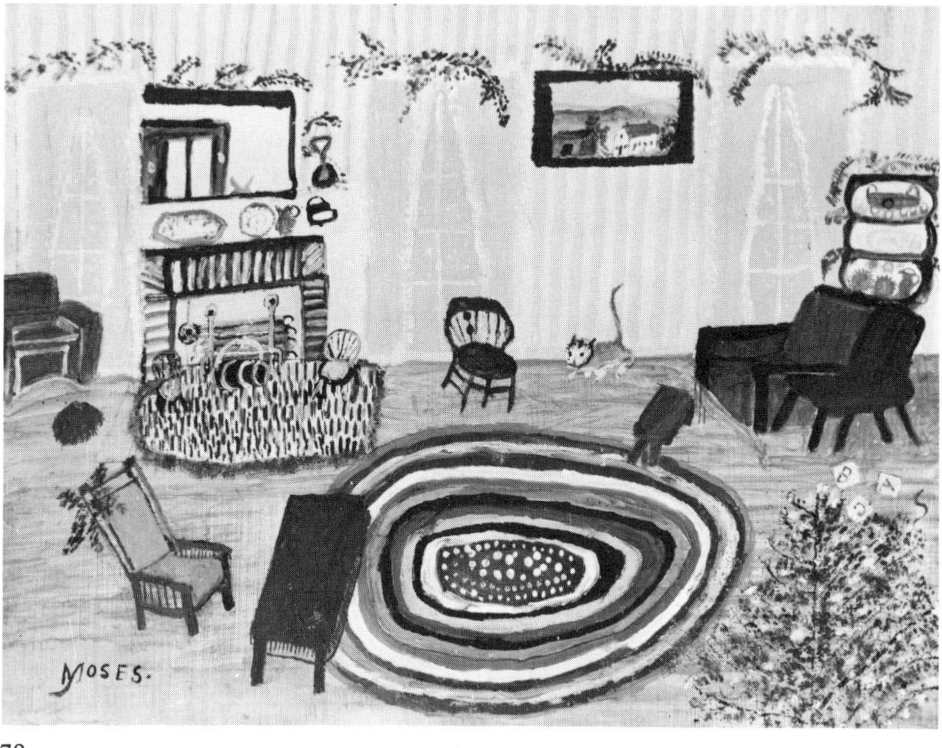

78

NIGHT BEFORE CHRISTMAS
1960

Loans to the New York Exhibition

CATALOGUE

LOANS TO THE NEW YORK EXHIBITION

82. HOME FOR THANKSGIVING (after the Currier and Ives print), ca. 1939. 10½ x 12½. Signed. *
83. BLACK HORSES, ca. 1942. 20 x 24. Signed. *
84. IT'S HAYING TIME, 1942. 21½ x 26. Signed. (GM 226)
85. HOME OF HEZEKIAH KING, 1943. 19 x 23½. Signed. (GM 331) * The Phoenix Art Museum, Phoenix, Arizona
86. MISSOURI, 1943. 20 x 23¾. Signed. (GM 340)
87. CATCHING THE THANKSGIVING TURKEY, 1943. 18½ x 24¼. Signed. (GM 353) * Collection of Mr. and Mrs. Henry S. McNeil
88. CAMBRIDGE VALLEY (RAIN IS COMING), 1943. 24 x 29¾. Signed. (GM 432)
89. MT. NEBO IN WINTER, 1943. 20½ x 26½. Signed. (GM 441) *
90. SUGARING OFF, 1943. 23 x 27. Signed. (GM 442) *
91. DECEMBER, 1943. 18½ x 22. Signed. (GM 449)
92. EVENING, 1943. 23¾ x 29¾. Signed. (GM 453)
93. McDONELL FARM, 1943. 24 x 30. Signed. (GM 518) *The Phillips Collection, Washington, D. C.
94. THE CHECKERED HOUSE IN SUMMER, 1944. 24 x 31¾. Signed. (GM 786) * Collection of Mr. and Mrs. Henry S. McNeil
95. CAMBRIDGE VALLEY IN WINTER, 1944. 23¾ x 29¾. Signed. (GM 1011) *
96. THE OLD AUTOMOBILE, 1944. 18¾ x 21½. Signed. (GM 1036) *
97. HOOSICK FALLS IN WINTER, 1944. 19½ x 24¾. Signed. (GM 1091) * The Abby Aldrich Rockefeller Folk Art Collection, Williamsburg, Virginia
98. WILD ROSES, 1945. 10¾ x 9¼. Signed. (GM 1022)
99. WILD DAISIES, 1945. 11¾ x 7¾. Signed. (GM 1022)
100. MY HILLS OF HOME, ca. 1946. Signed. Memorial Art Gallery, Rochester, New York
101. GRANDMA GOES TO NEW YORK, 1946. 36 x 48. Signed. Oil on canvas. (GM 1094) *
102. CHRISTMAS AT HOME, 1946. 18 x 23. Signed. (GM 1103) *
103. THE LONE TRAVELER, 1946. 16 x 19¾. Signed. (GM 1111)

104. A TRAMP ON CHRISTMAS DAY, 1946. 16 x 20. Signed. (GM 1112)* Courtesy Webb Gallery of American Art, Shelburne Museum, Shelburne, Vermont
105. HOW THE WIND BLOWS, 1946. 16 x 19¾. Signed. (GM 1113)
106. OUT FOR THE CHRISTMAS TREES, 1946. 26 x 36. Signed. (GM 1118) *
107. HOOSICK VALLEY FROM MY WINDOW, 1946. 19½ x 22. Signed. (GM 1123) *
108. THE OLD OAKEN BUCKET, 1946. 24 x 28½. Signed. (GM 1127) * Collection of Mr. and Mrs. John M. Schiff, New York
109. NO SKATING FOR ME, 1946. 27 x 21. Signed. (GM 1144) Collection of Mr. and Mrs. John M. Schiff, New York
110. THE BLACK BUGGY (COVERED BRIDGE WITH CARRIAGE), 1946. 27½ x 21½. Signed. (GM 1158) Courtesy Webb Gallery of American Art, Shelburne Museum, Shelburne, Vermont
111. LITTLE BOY BLUE, 1947. 20½ x 23. Signed. (GM 1170) *
112. THE DIVIDING OF THE WAYS, 1947. 16 x 20. Signed. (GM 1206) *
113. SPRING IN EVENING, 1947. 27 x 21. Signed (GM 1211) *
114. FOR THIS IS THE FALL OF THE YEAR, 1947. 16 x 21¾. Signed. (GM 1216)
115. JACK AND JILL, 1947. 12½ x 19¾. Signed. (GM 1224)
116. THUNDERSTORM, 1948. 20¾ x 24¾. Signed. (GM 1227) *
117. THE HITCHING POST, 1948. 15 x 19¼. Signed. (GM 1285)
118. HAYING IN VERMONT, 1948. 16 x 24. Signed. (GM 1294) Collection of Mr. and Mrs. Rudolf Bing, New York
119. THE MAILMAN HAS GONE, 1949. 16¾ x 21½. Signed. (GM 1319) * Courtesy Webb Gallery of American Art, Shelburne Museum, Shelburne, Vermont
120. GRANDMOTHER, 1950. 20 x 23½. Signed. (GM 1373) Collection of Mr. and Mrs. John M. Schiff, New York
121. WHEN THE LEAVES HAVE FALLEN, 1950. 20 x 24. Signed. Oil on canvas. (GM 1406) *
122. COUNTRY FAIR, 1950. 35 x 45. Signed. Oil on canvas. (GM 1417) *
123. TAKING IN LAUNDRY, 1951. 17 x 21¾. Signed. (GM 1458) *
124. WE ARE RESTING, 1951. 24 x 30. Signed. (GM 1461) *
125. HUSKING BEE, 1951. 19 x 24. Signed. (GM 1478) *
126. THE RAINBOW, 1951. 20 x 24. Signed. (GM 1495) *
127. A BEAUTIFUL MORNING, 1951. 18 x 24. Signed. (GM 1501) Collection of Mr. and Mrs. Henry S. McNeil
128. HOOSICK RIVER, WINTER. 1952. 18 x 24. Signed. (GM 1522) *
129. HOOSICK RIVER, SUMMER. 1952. 18 x 24. Signed. (GM 1523) *
130. NEW SNOW, 1952. 18 x 24. Signed. (GM 1533)
131. BUSY STREET, 1952. 18 x 24. Signed. (GM 1545) Courtesy Hallmark Cards, Incorporated, Kansas City
132. DARK SKY, 1953. 18 x 24. Signed. (GM 1558) *
133. JOY RIDE, 1953. 18 x 24. Signed. (GM 1569) *

134. WHITE CHRISTMAS, 1954. 19¾ x 23¾. Signed. (GM 1651) *
Collection of Mr. Irving Berlin, New York

135. HALLOWEEN, 1955. 18 x 24. Signed. (GM 1677) *

136. HELP, 1956. 16 x 24. Signed. (GM 1724) *

137. SNOWED IN, 1957. 12 x 16. Signed. (GM 1762) *

138. LONG LAKE, 1958. 18 x 24. Signed. (GM 1826)

139. BIRCHES, 1958. 16 x 24. Signed. (GM 1829)

140. DARK MORNING, 1959. 16 x 24. Signed. (GM 1868)

141. SKIING, 1959. 16 x 24. Signed. (GM 1869)

142. SNOW BALLS, 1959. 16 x 24. Signed. (GM 1870)

143. MORNING, 1959. 16 x 24. Signed. (GM 1872)

144. NOON TIME, 1959. 16 x 24. Signed. (GM 1900) *

145. GREAT FIRE, 1959. 12 x 16. Signed, and inscribed "The Burning of Troy in 1862" (GM 1911) *

146. AUTUMN LEAVES, 1959. 16 x 24. Signed. (GM 1923) *

147. SUGARING OFF, 1960 (unfinished). 16 x 24. (GM 1943) *

148. WHITE BIRCHES, 1961. 16 x 24. Signed. (GM 1991)*

149. RAINBOW, 1961. 16 x 24. Signed. (GM 1997)

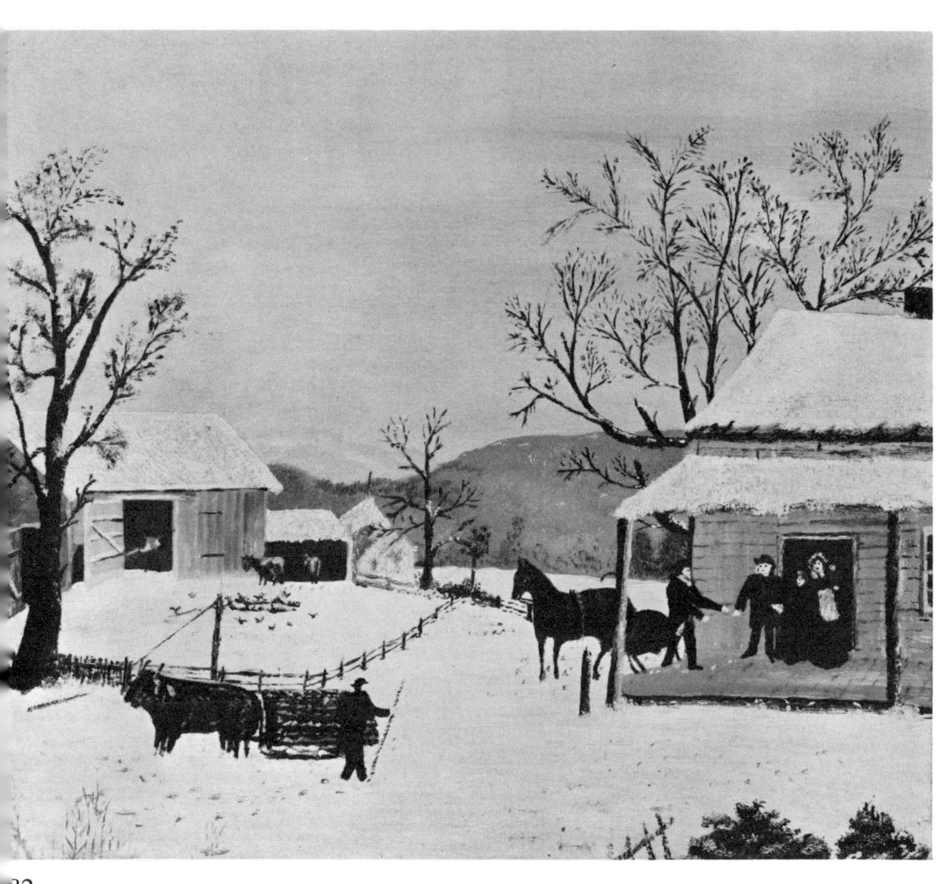

82

HOME FOR THANKSGIVING. ca. 1939
(After the Currier and Ives print)

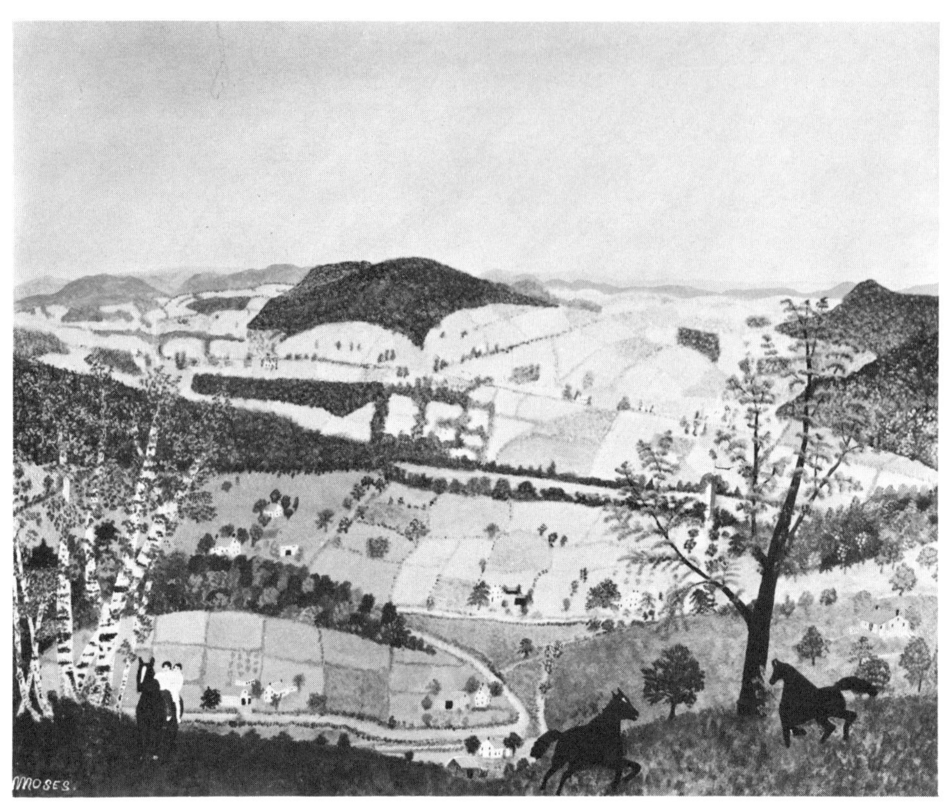

83

BLACK HORSES. ca. 1942

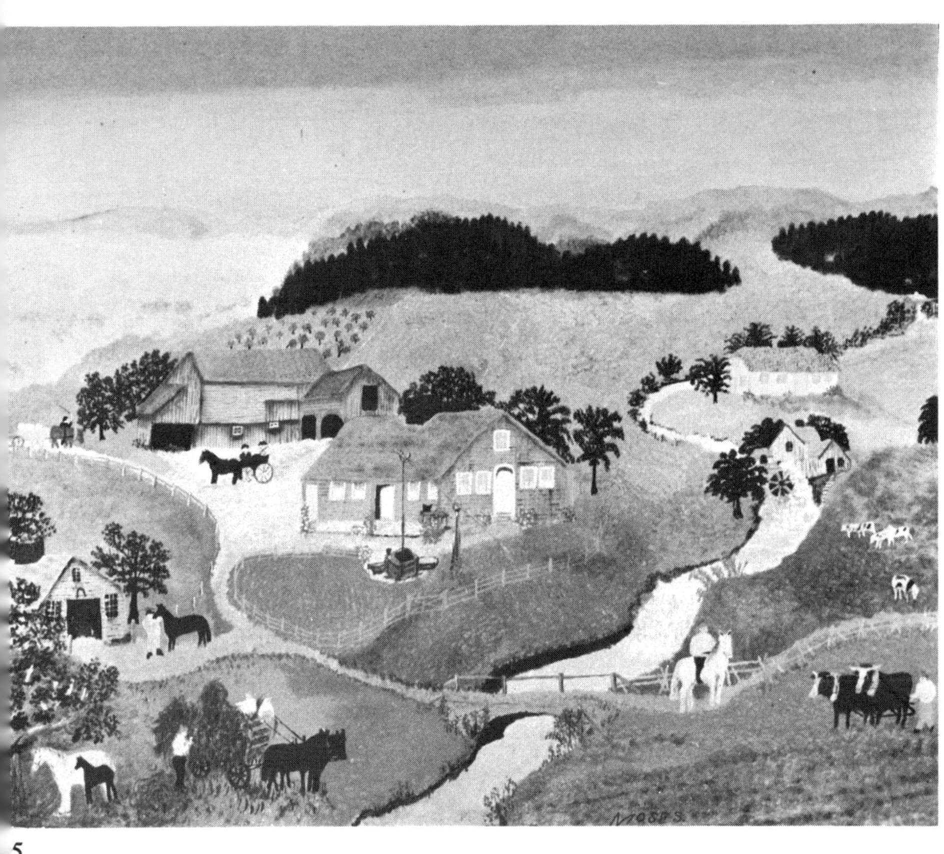

5

HOME OF HEZEKIAH KING IN 1776. 1943

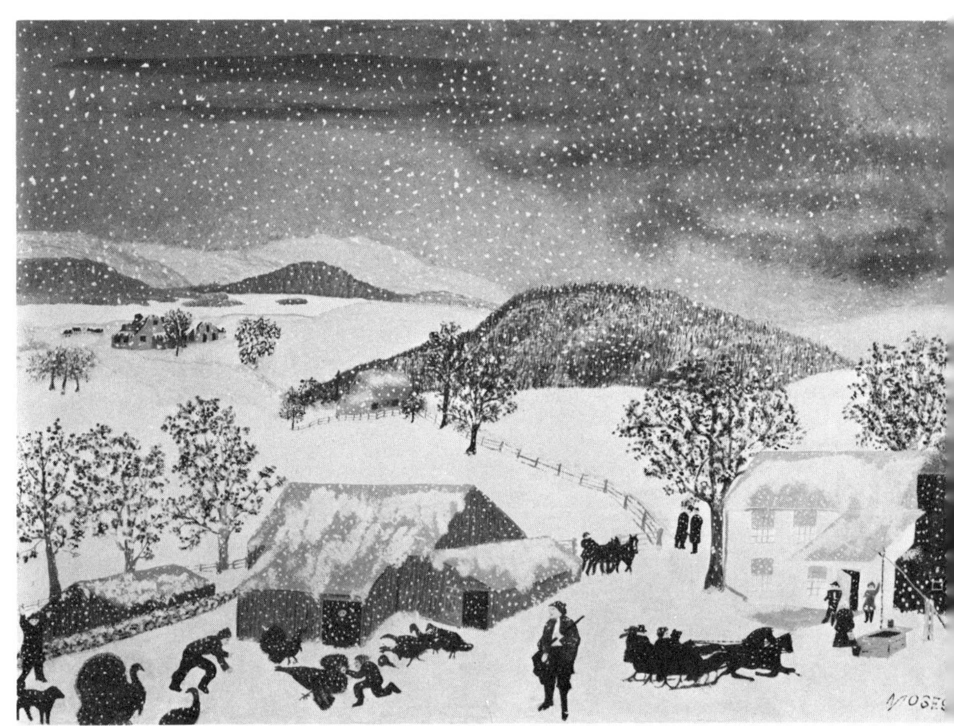

87

CATCHING THE THANKSGIVING TURKEY. 1943

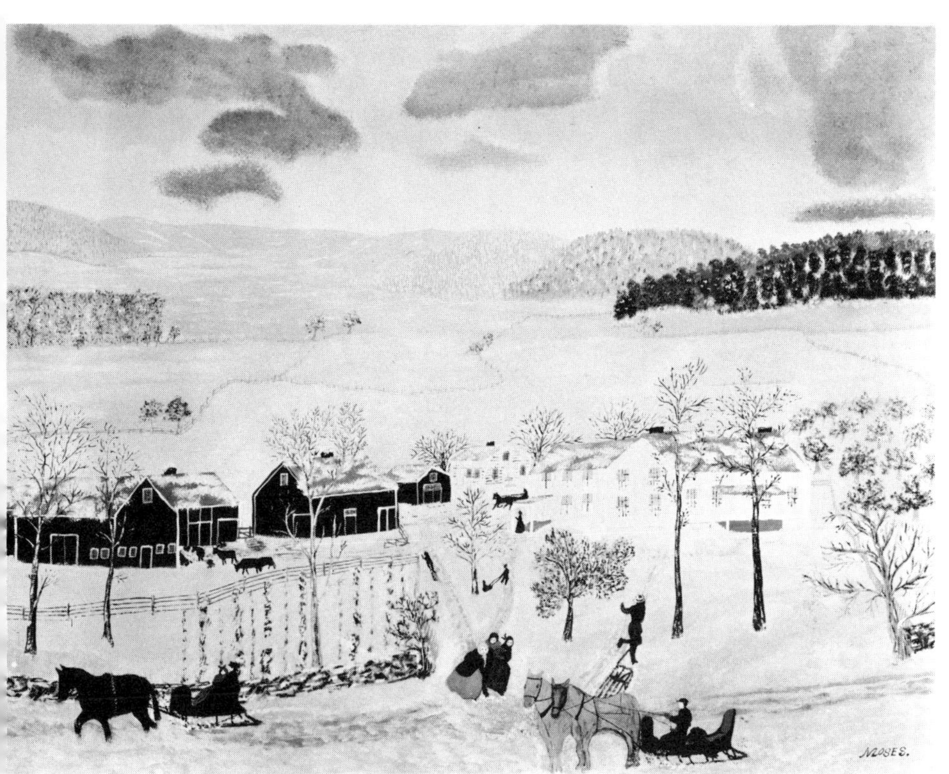

89

MT. NEBO IN WINTER. 1943

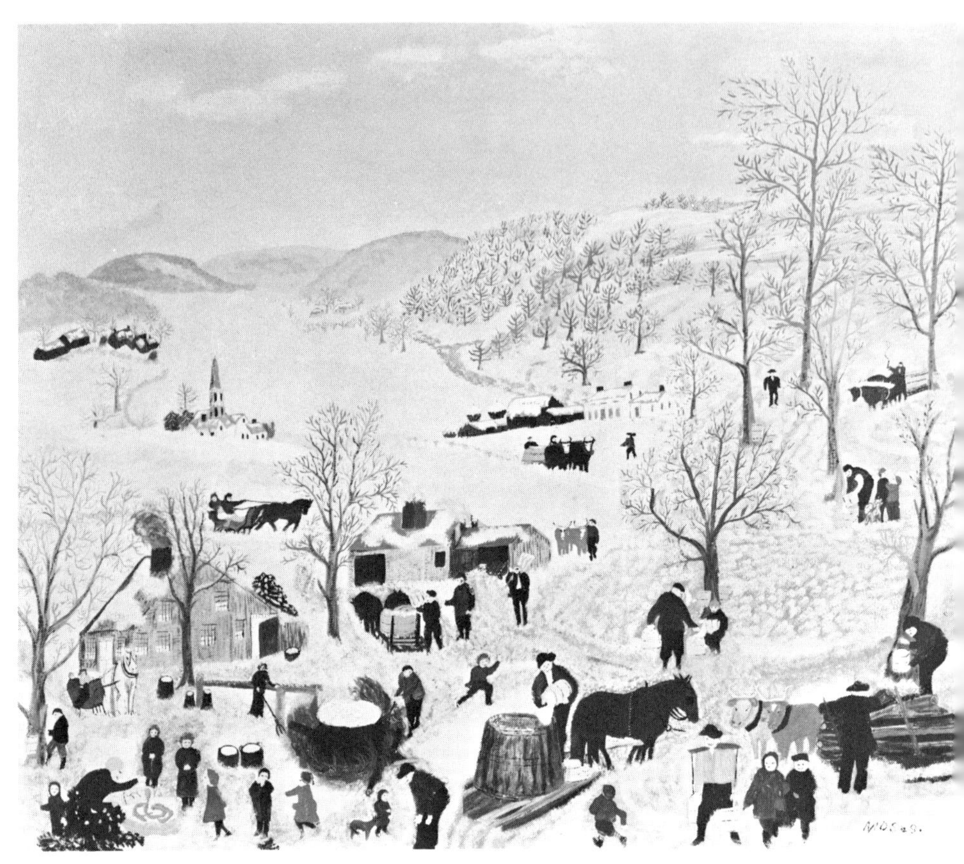

90

SUGARING OFF. 1943

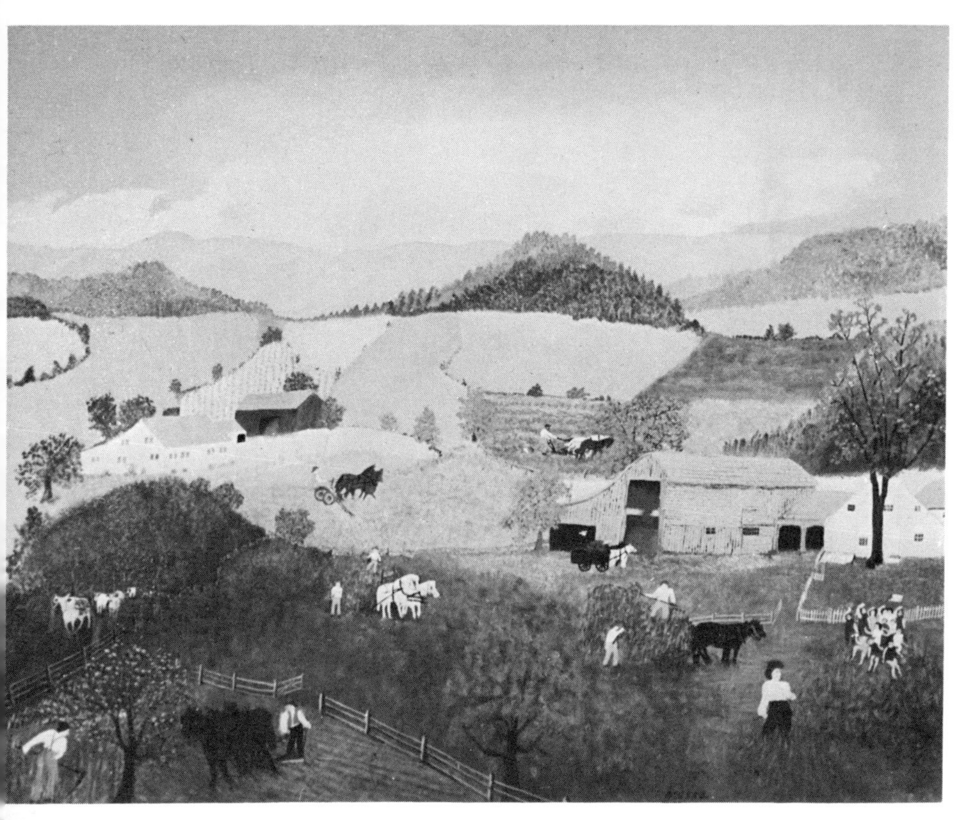

93

McDONELL FARM. 1943

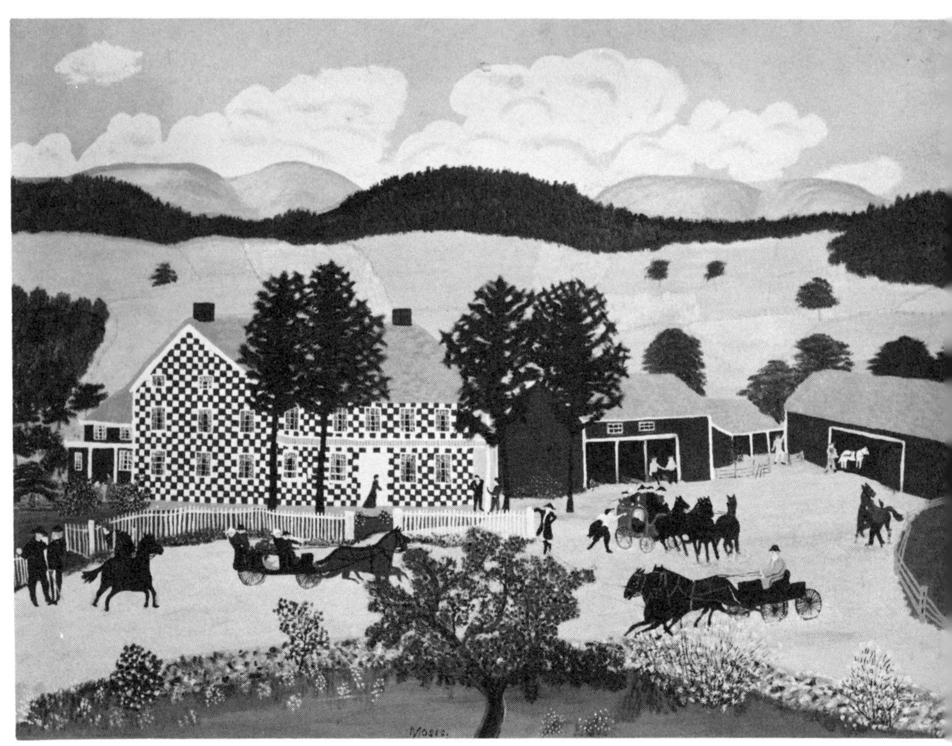

94

THE CHECKERED HOUSE IN SUMMER. 1944

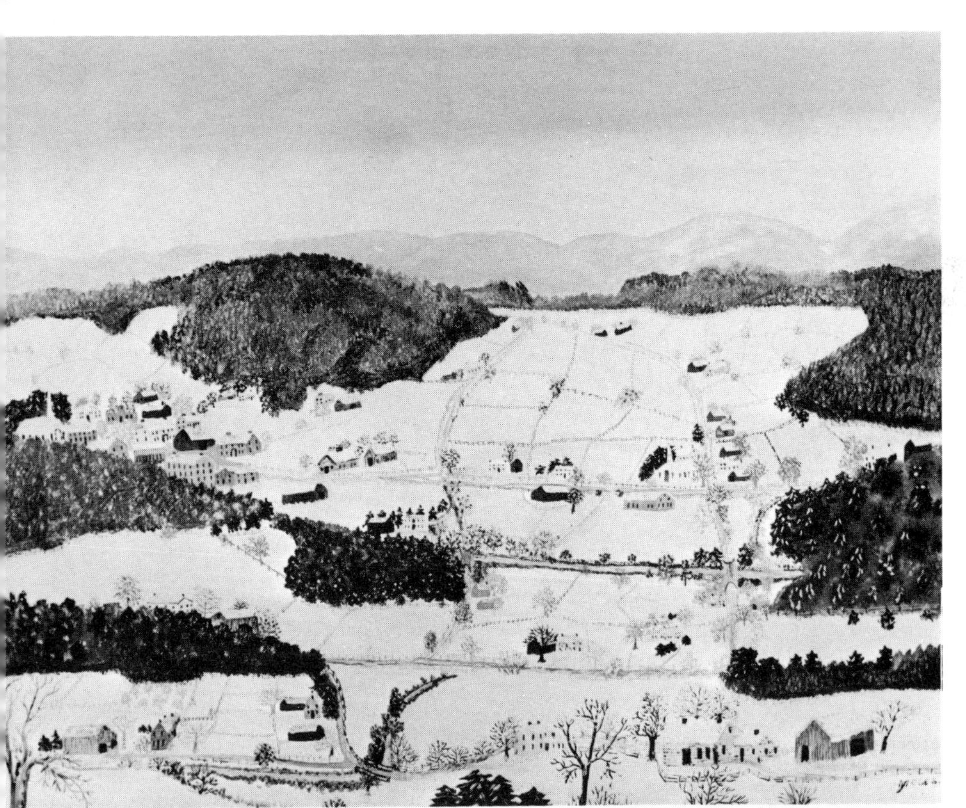

95

CAMBRIDGE VALLEY IN WINTER. 1944

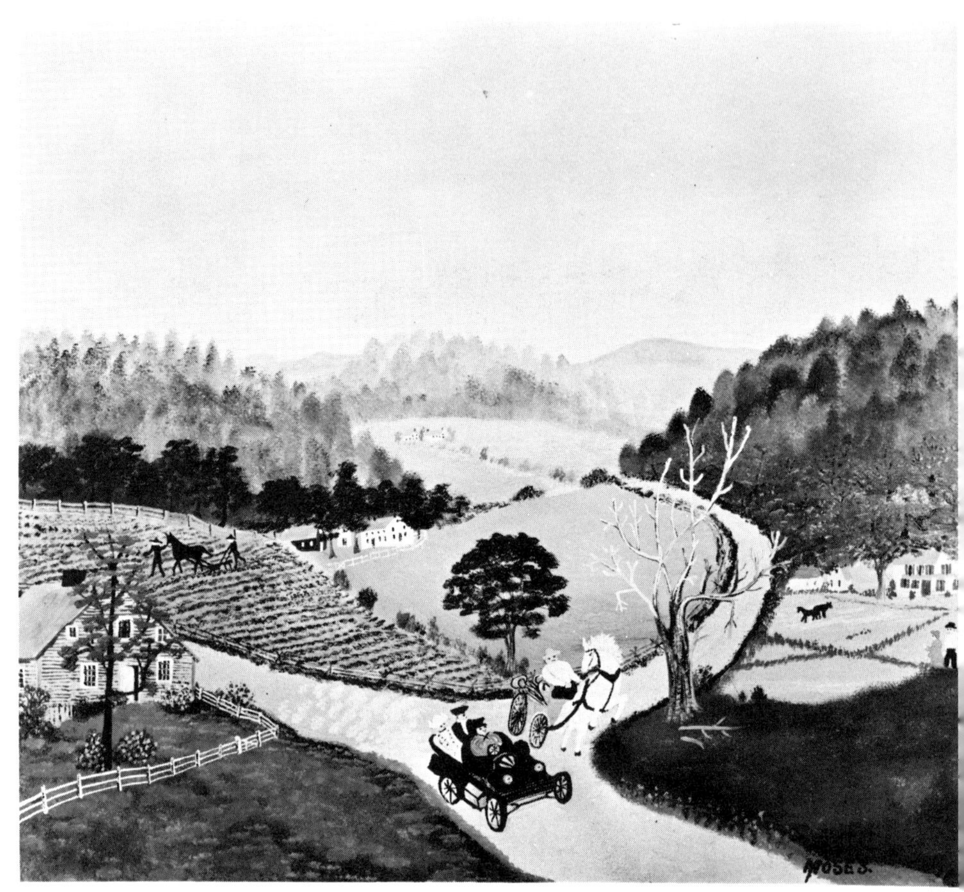

96

THE OLD AUTOMOBILE. 1944

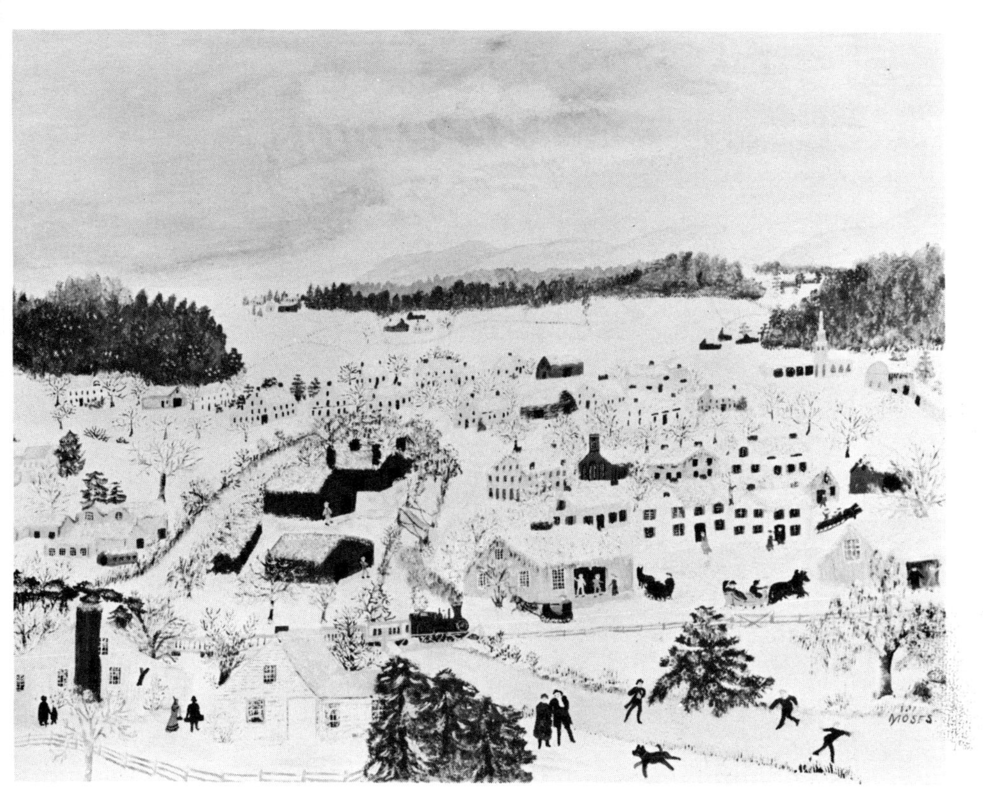

97

HOOSICK FALLS IN WINTER. 1944

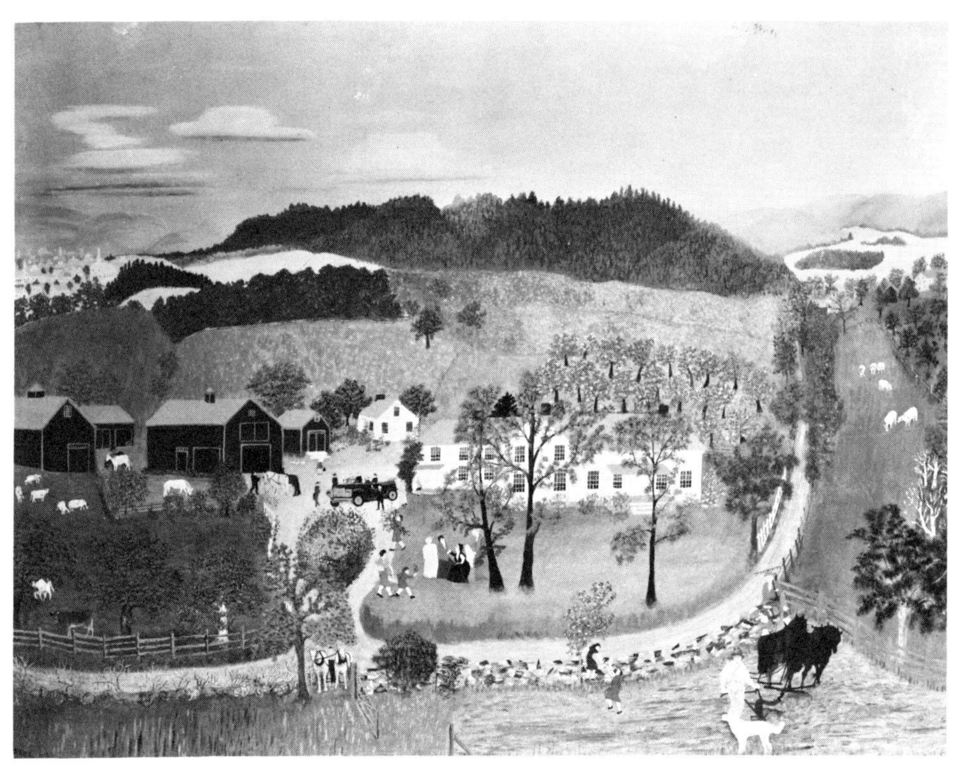

101

GRANDMA GOES TO NEW YORK. 1946

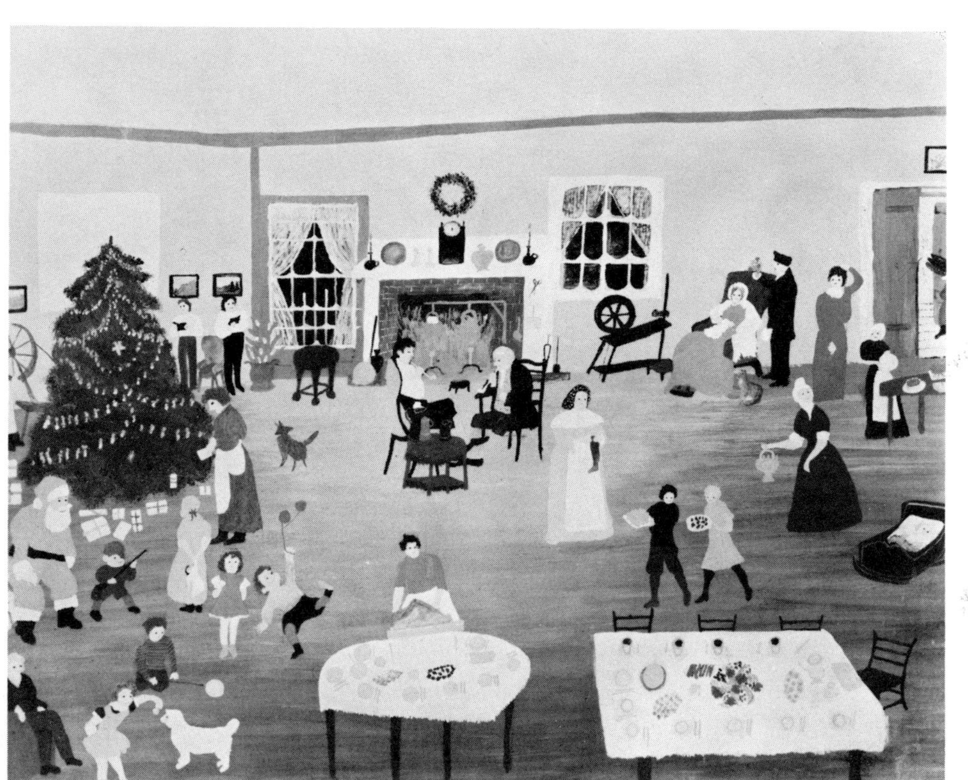

102

CHRISTMAS AT HOME. 1946

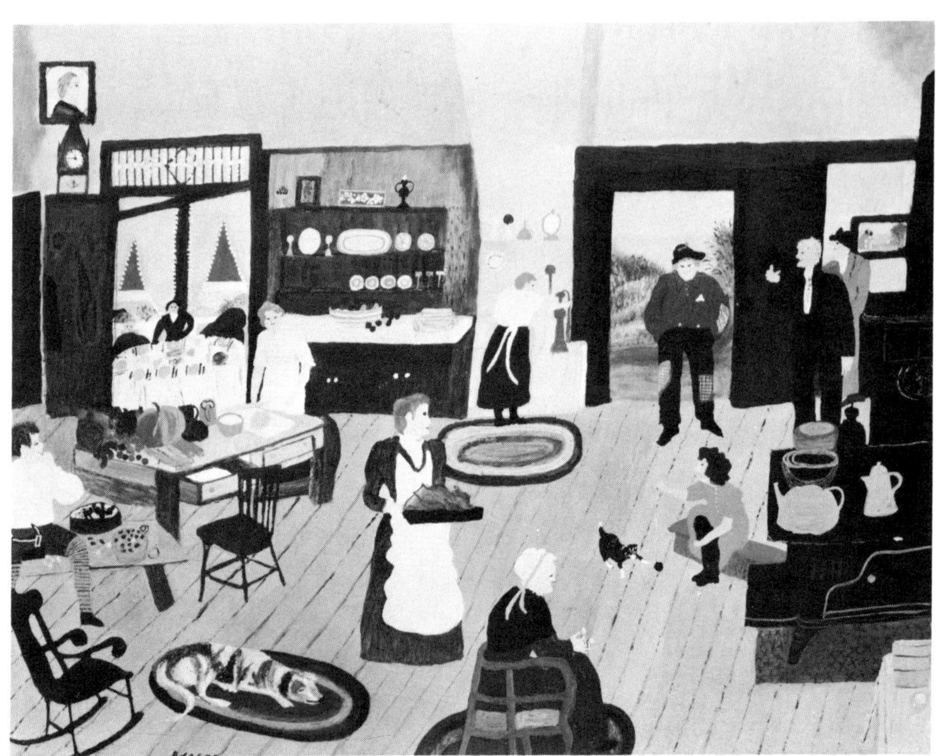

104

A TRAMP ON CHRISTMAS DAY. 1946

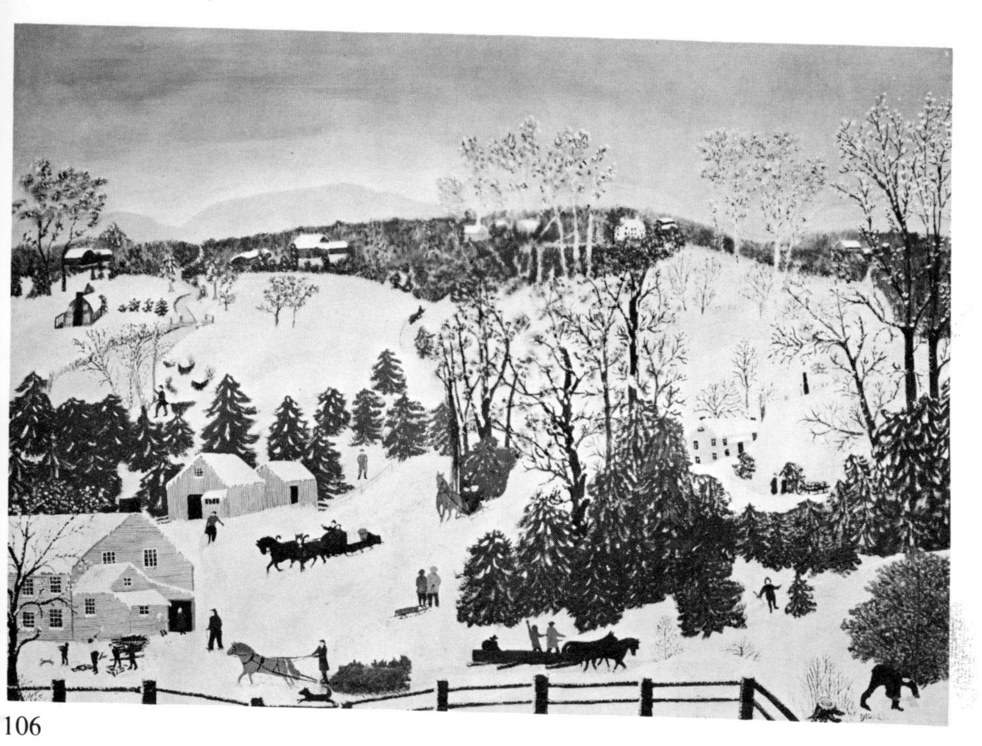

106

OUT FOR THE CHRISTMAS TREES. 1946

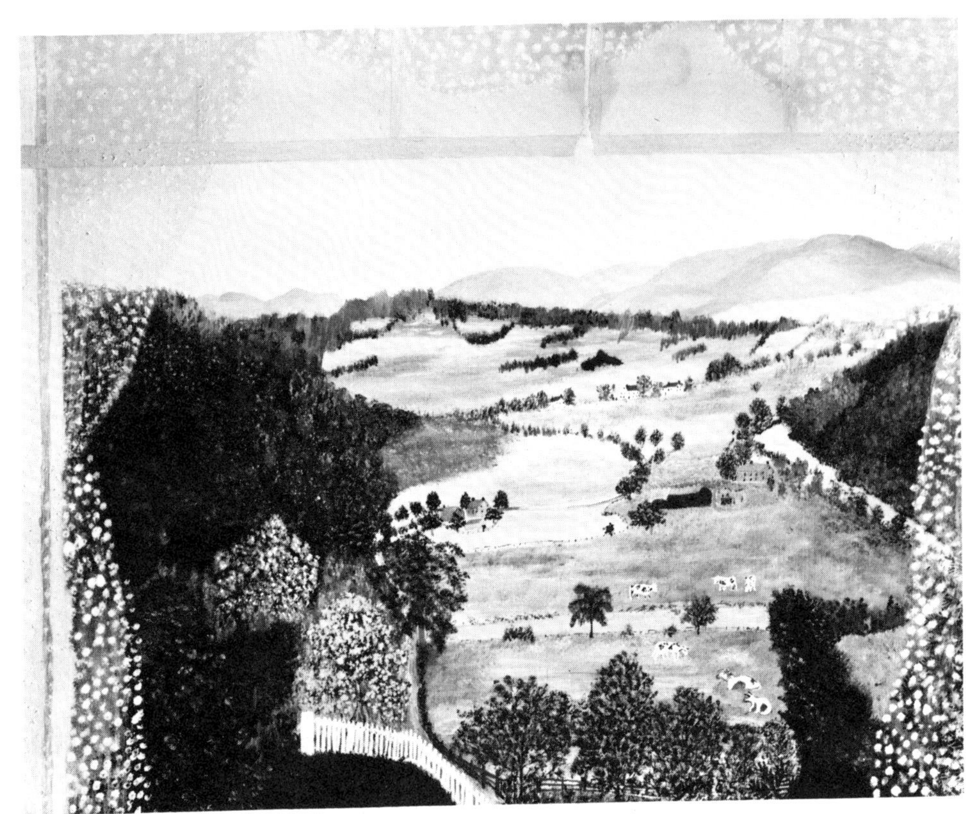

107

HOOSICK VALLEY FROM MY WINDOW. 1946

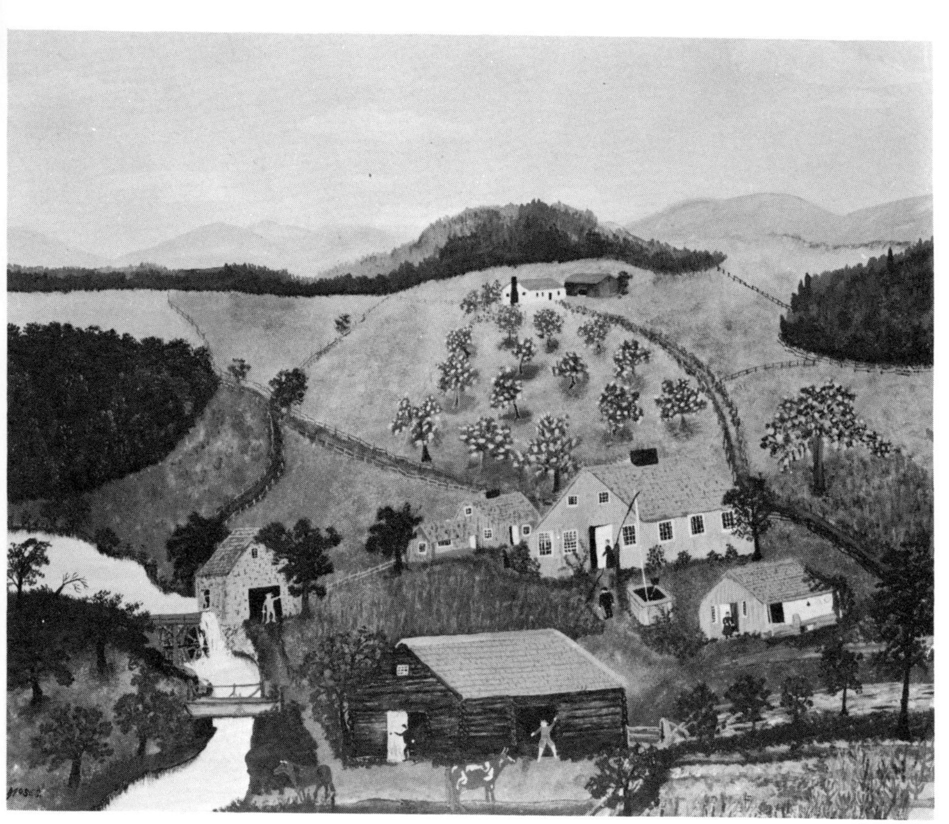

108

THE OLD OAKEN BUCKET. 1946

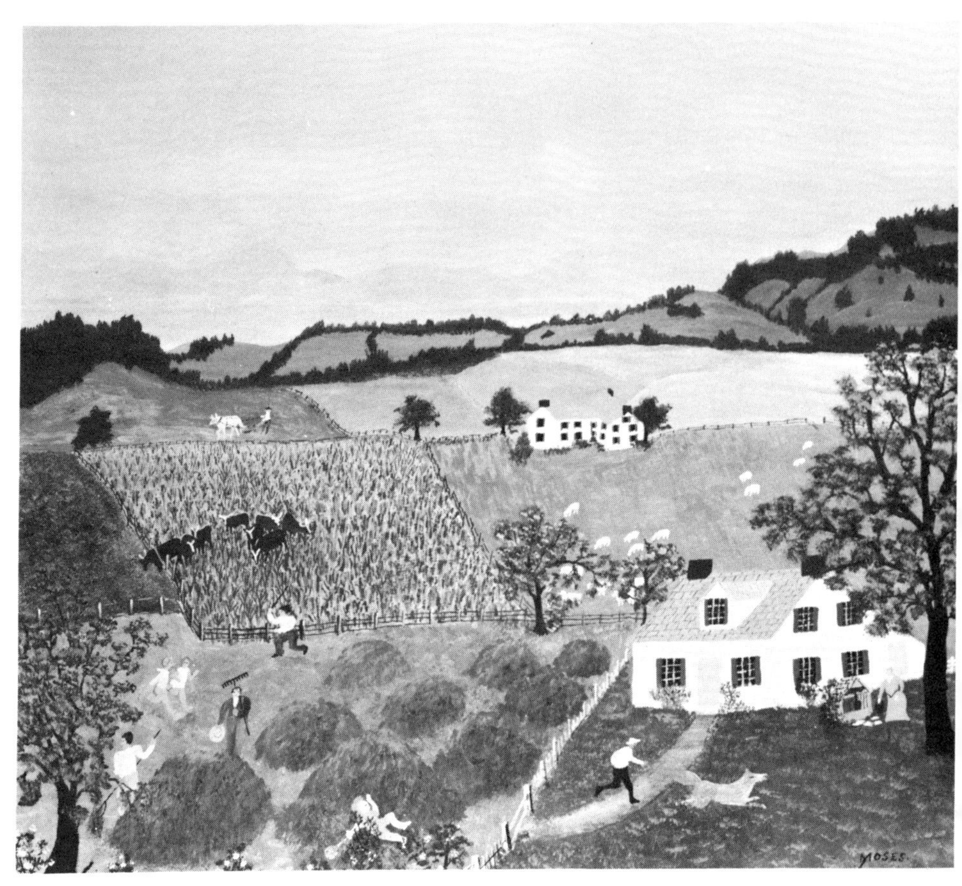

111

LITTLE BOY BLUE. 1947

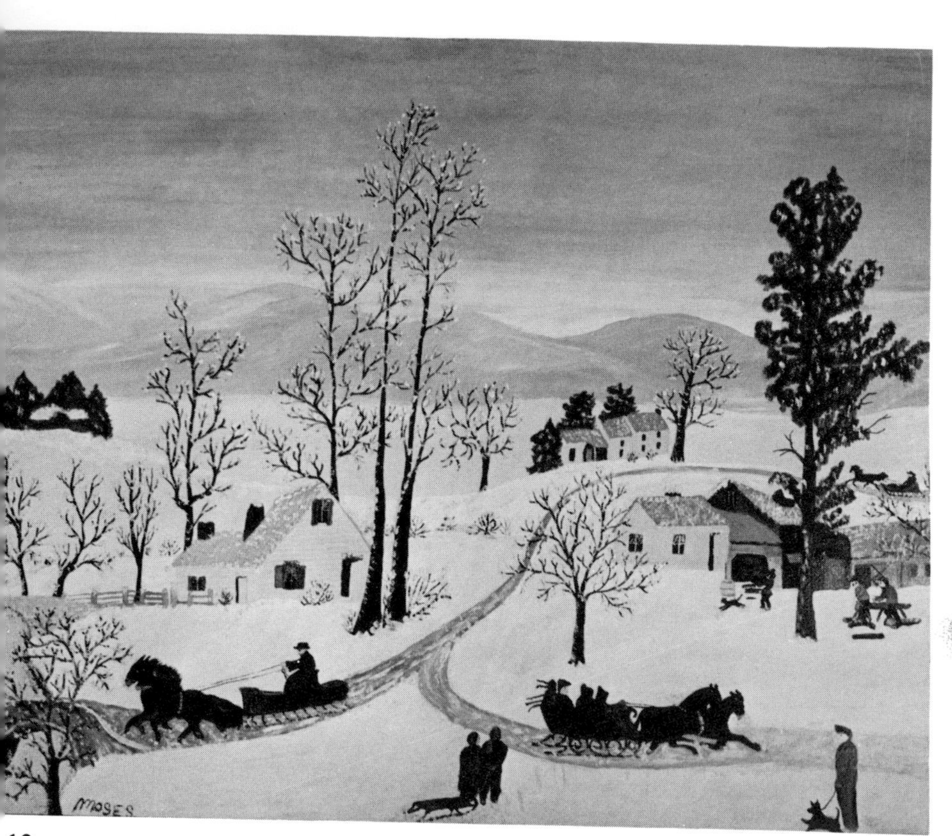

12

THE DIVIDING OF THE WAYS. 1947

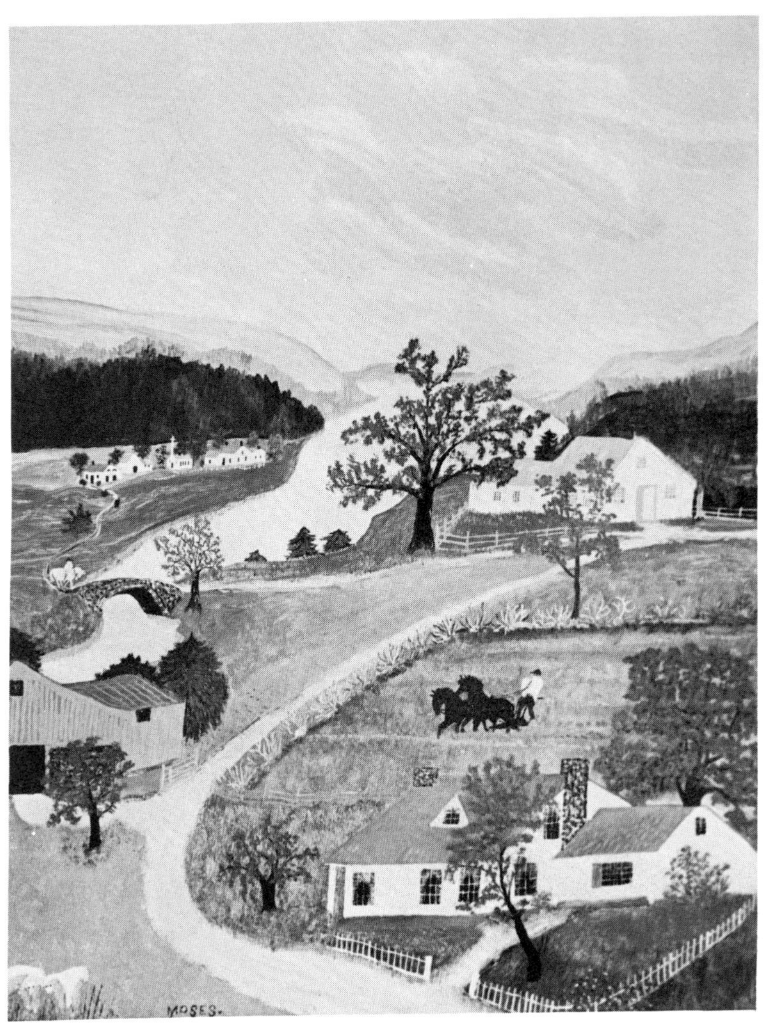

113

SPRING IN EVENING. 1947

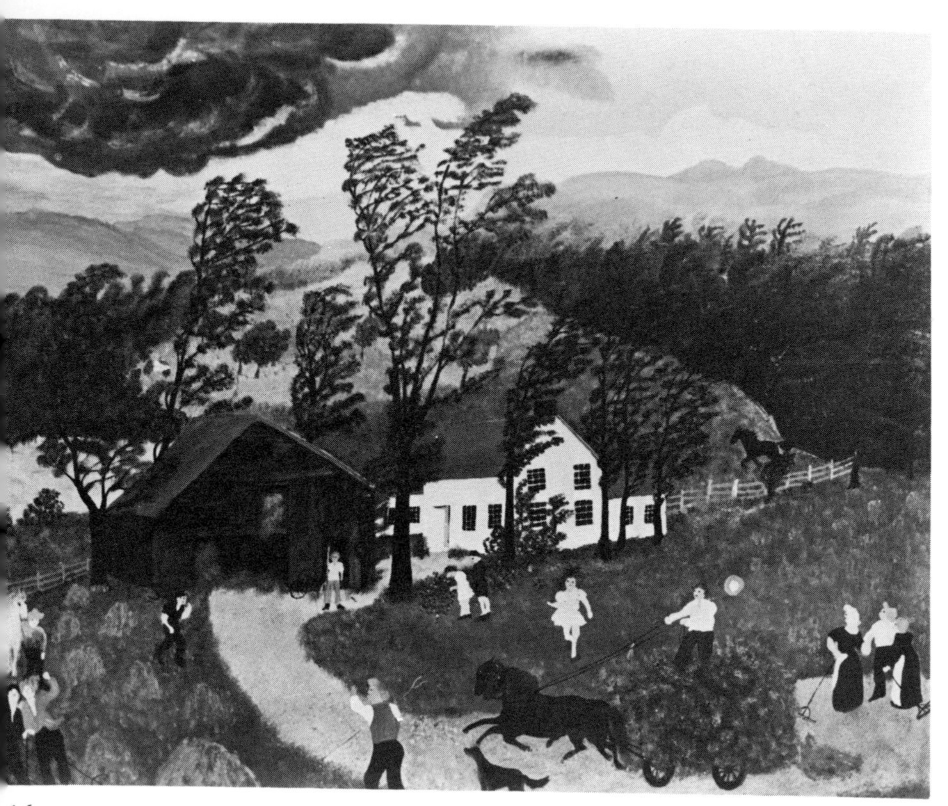

16

THUNDERSTORM. 1948

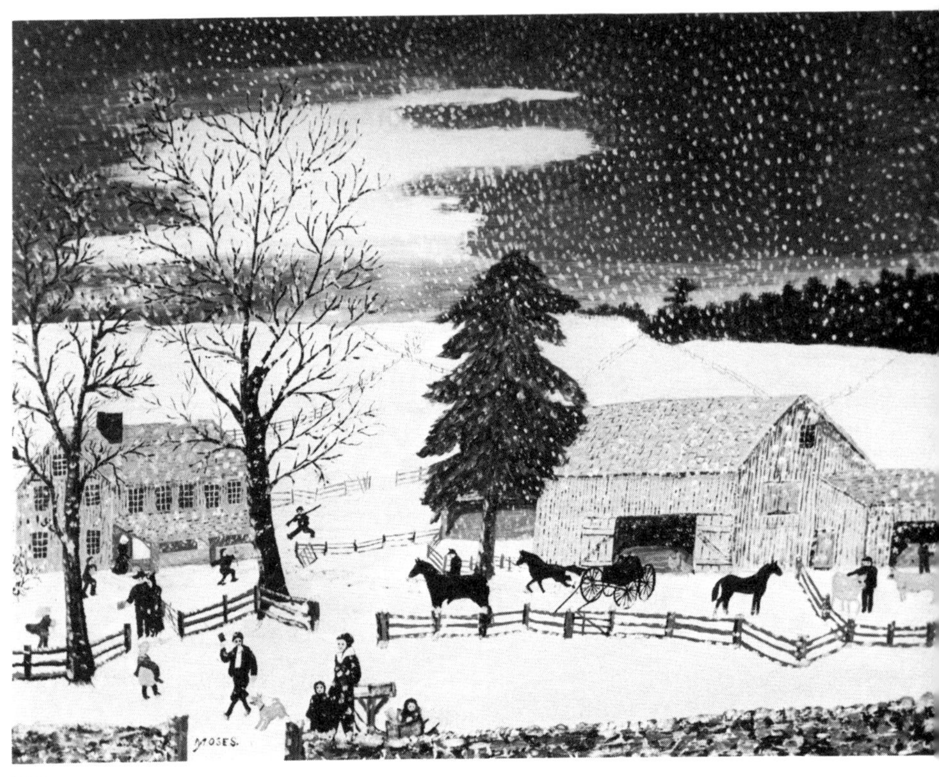

119

THE MAILMAN HAS GONE. 1949

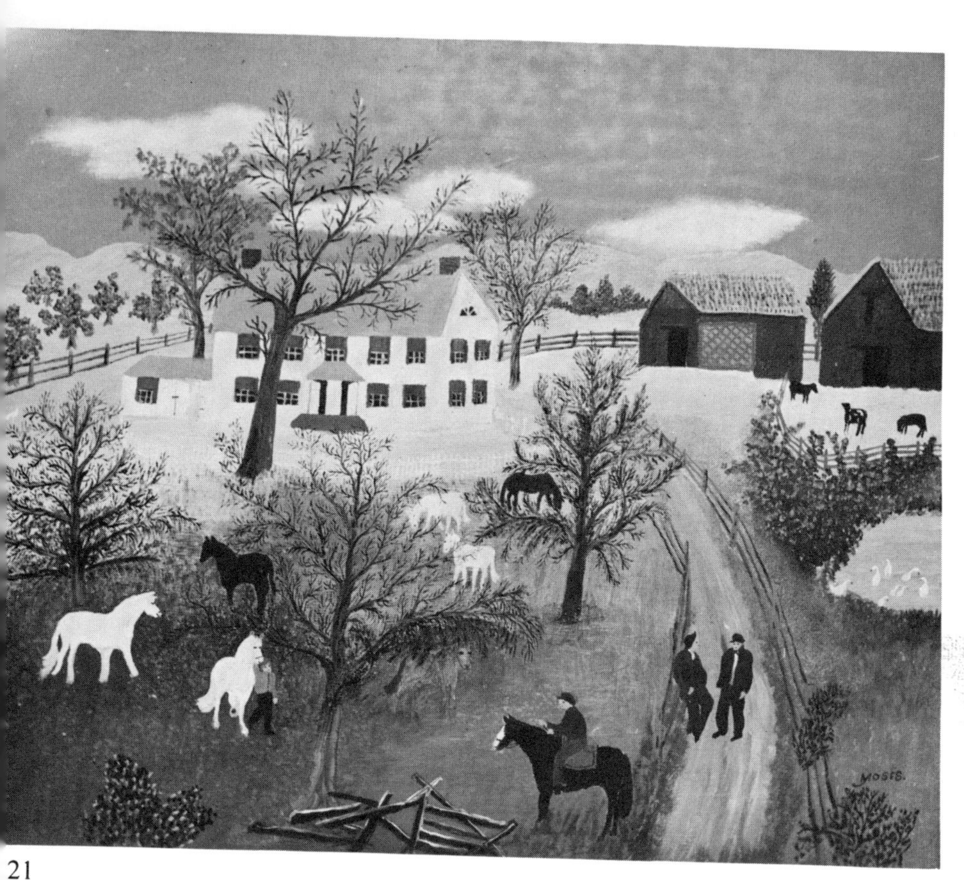

21

WHEN THE LEAVES HAVE FALLEN. 1950

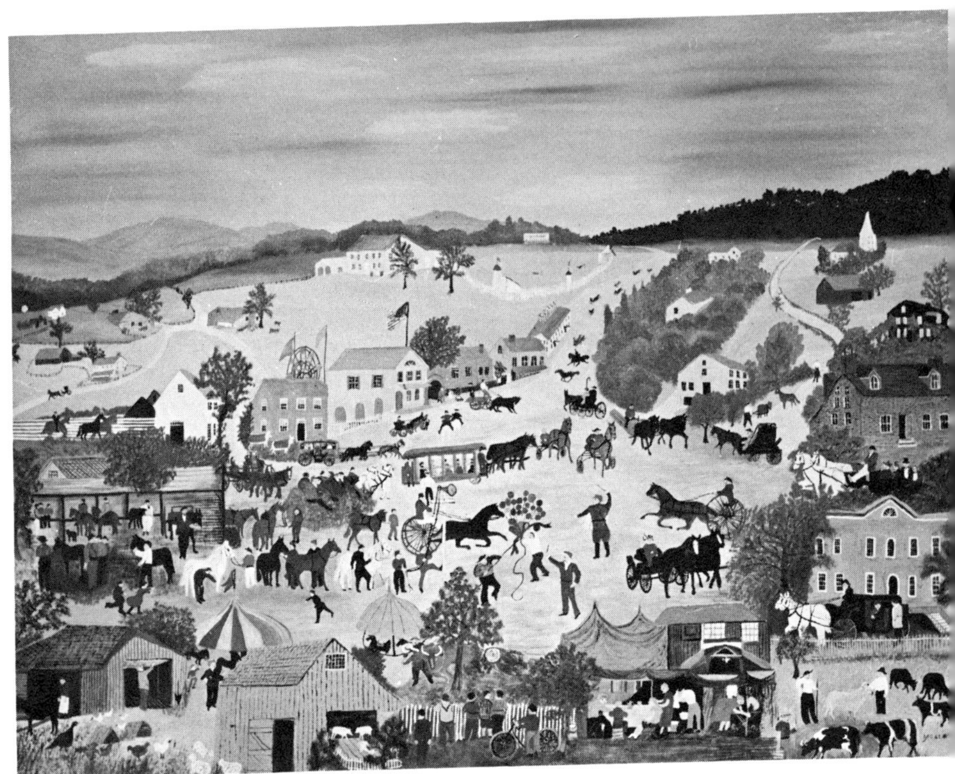

122

COUNTRY FAIR. 1950

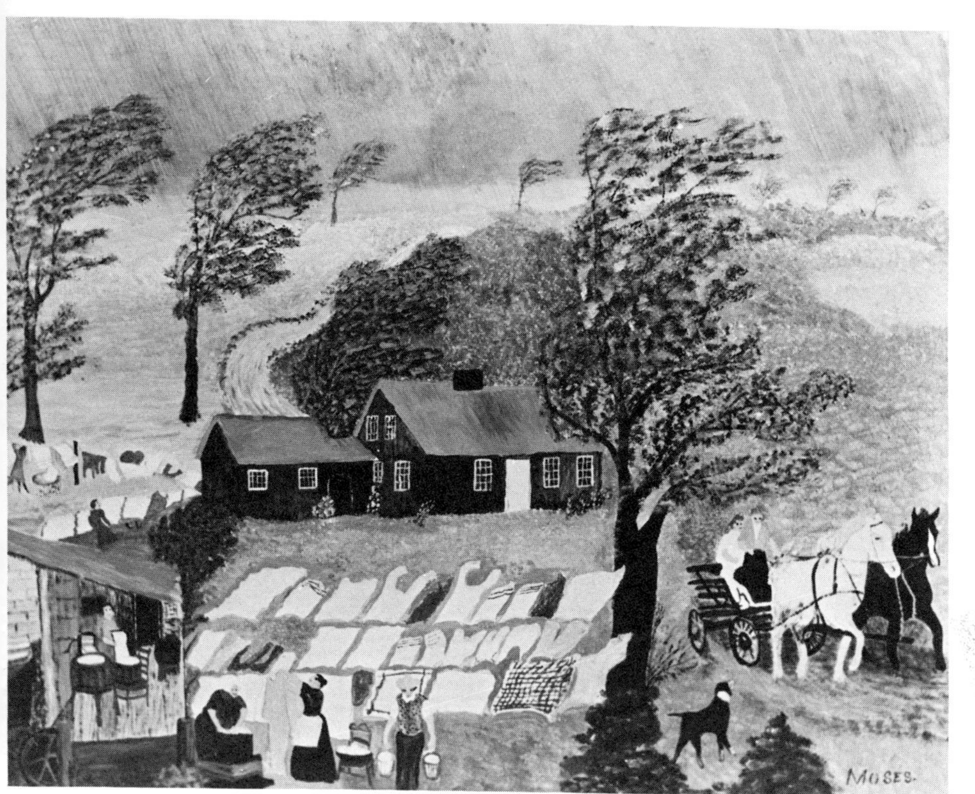

123

TAKING IN LAUNDRY. 1951

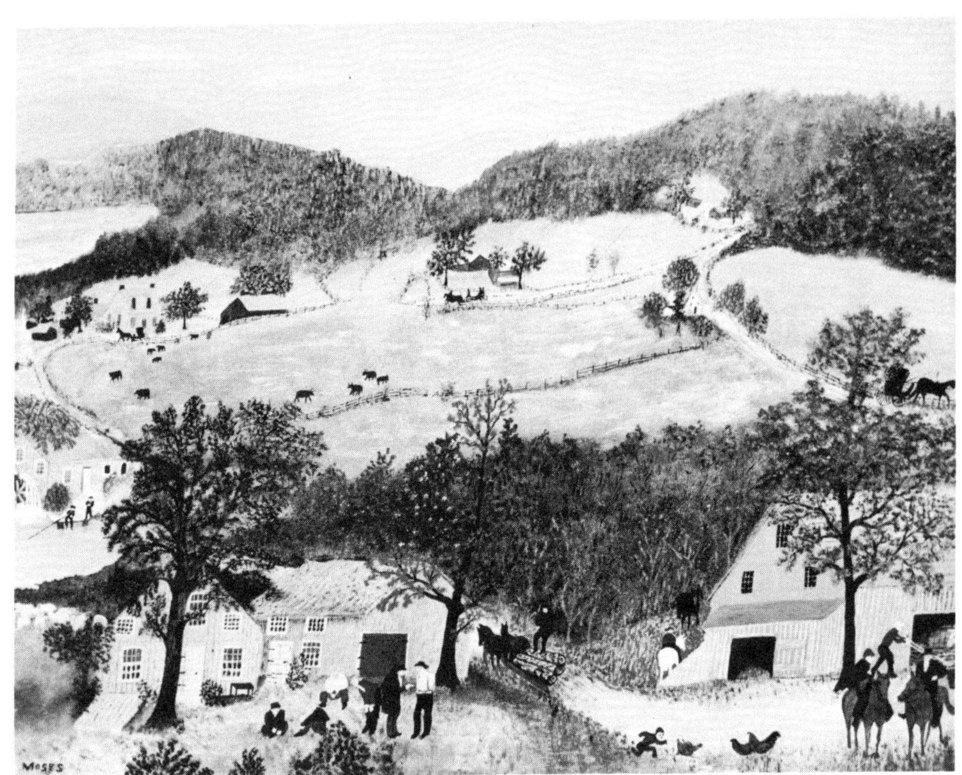

124

WE ARE RESTING. 1951

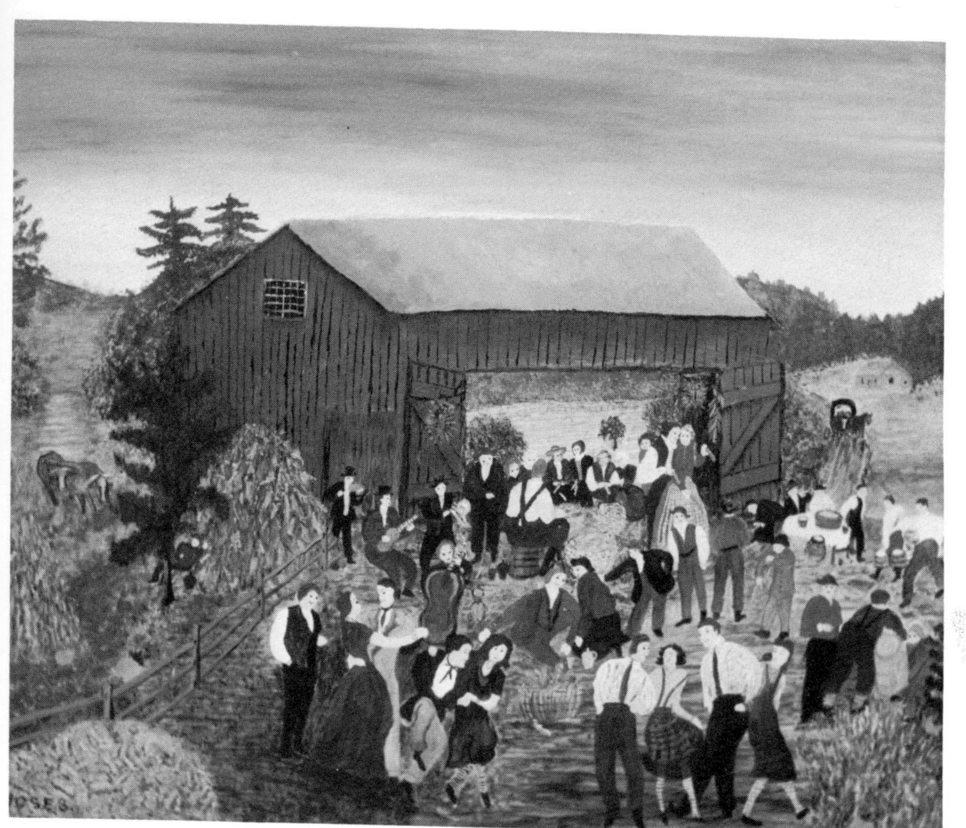

125

HUSKING BEE. 1951

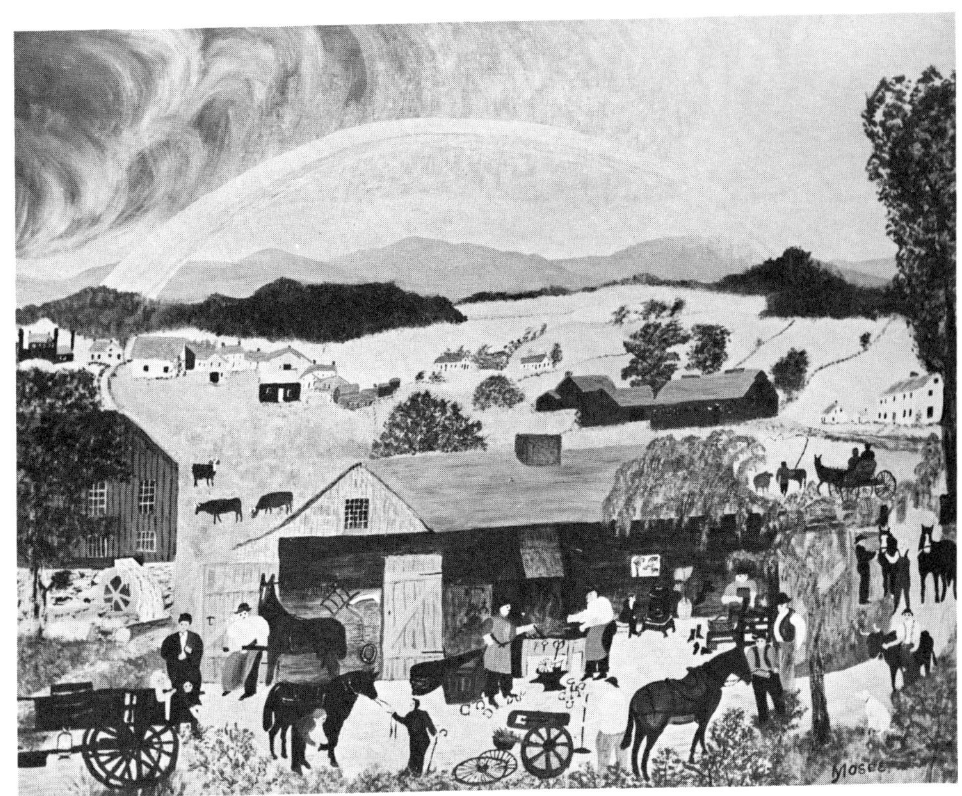

126

THE RAINBOW. 1951

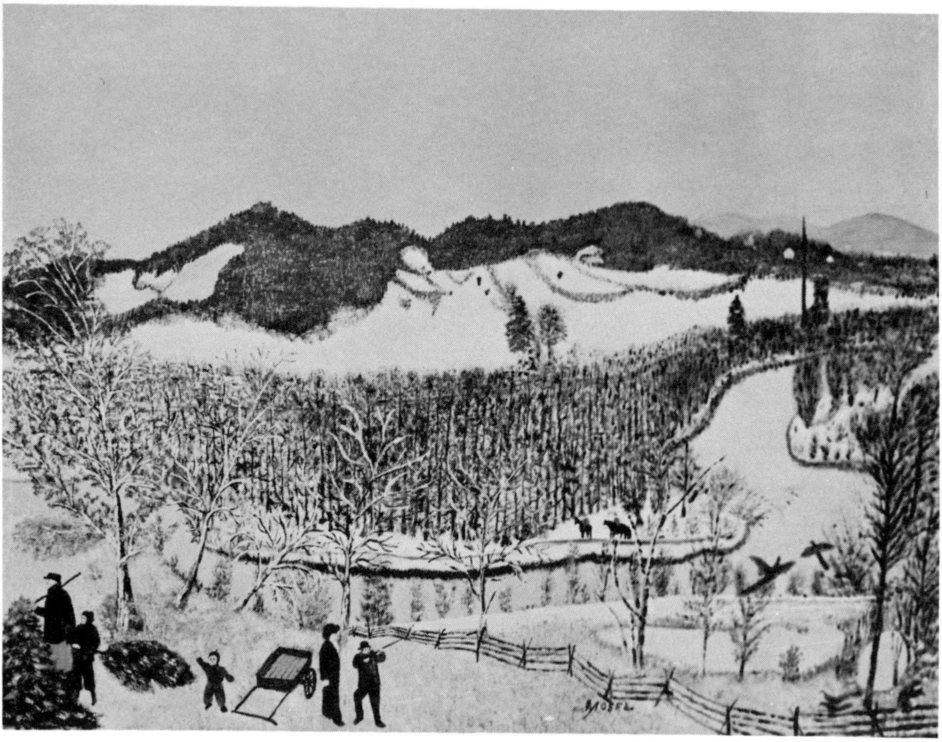

128 HOOSICK RIVER IN WINTER. 1952

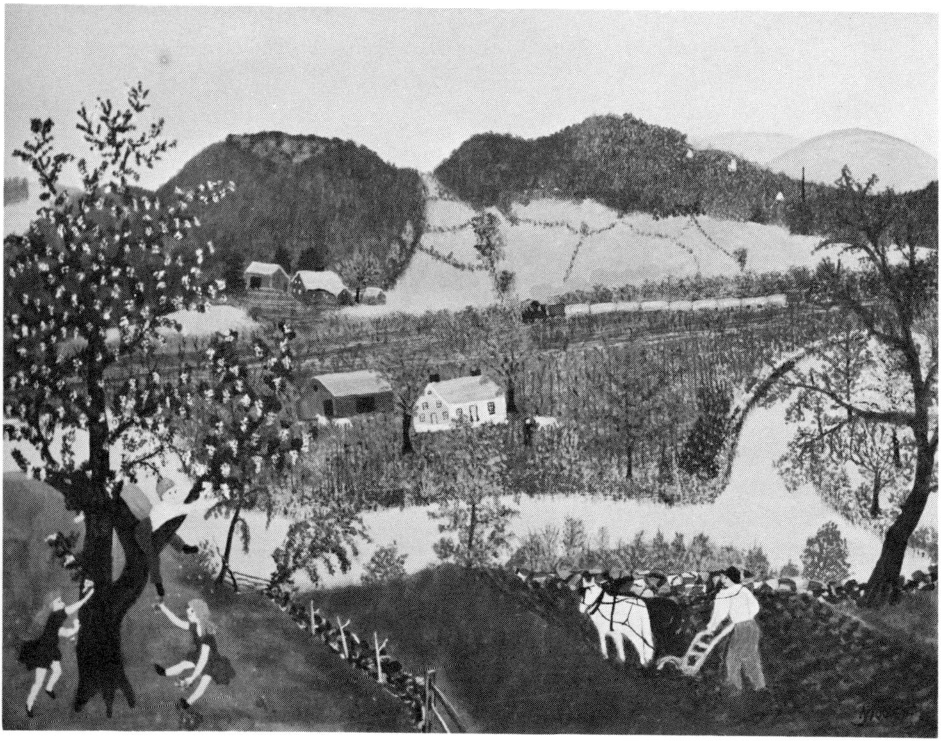

129 HOOSICK RIVER IN SUMMER. 1952

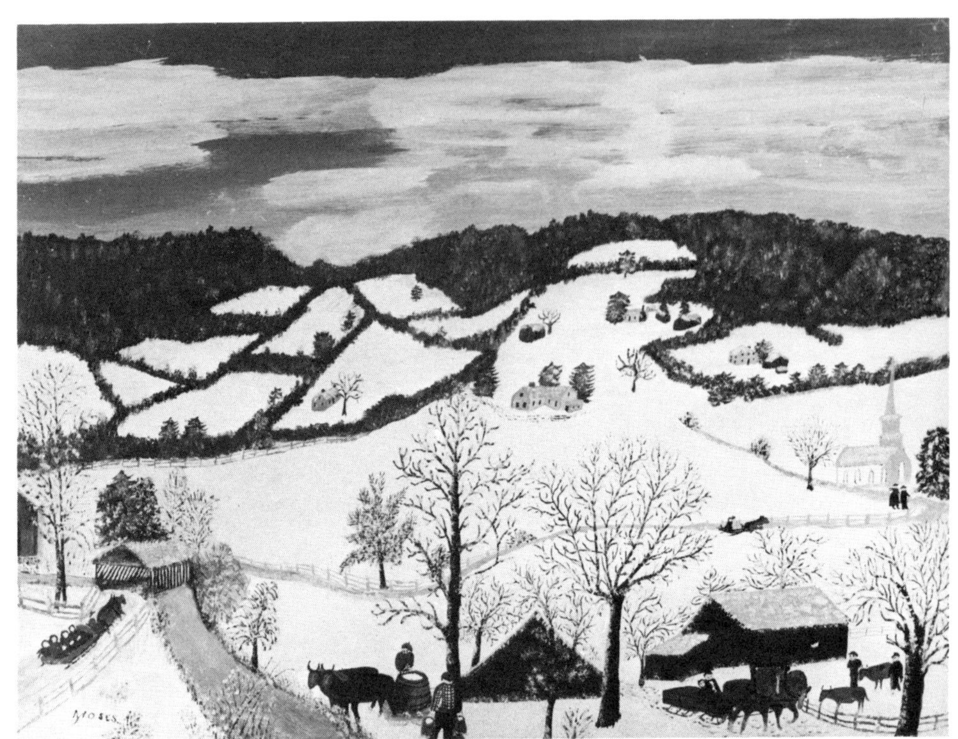

132

DARK SKY. 1953

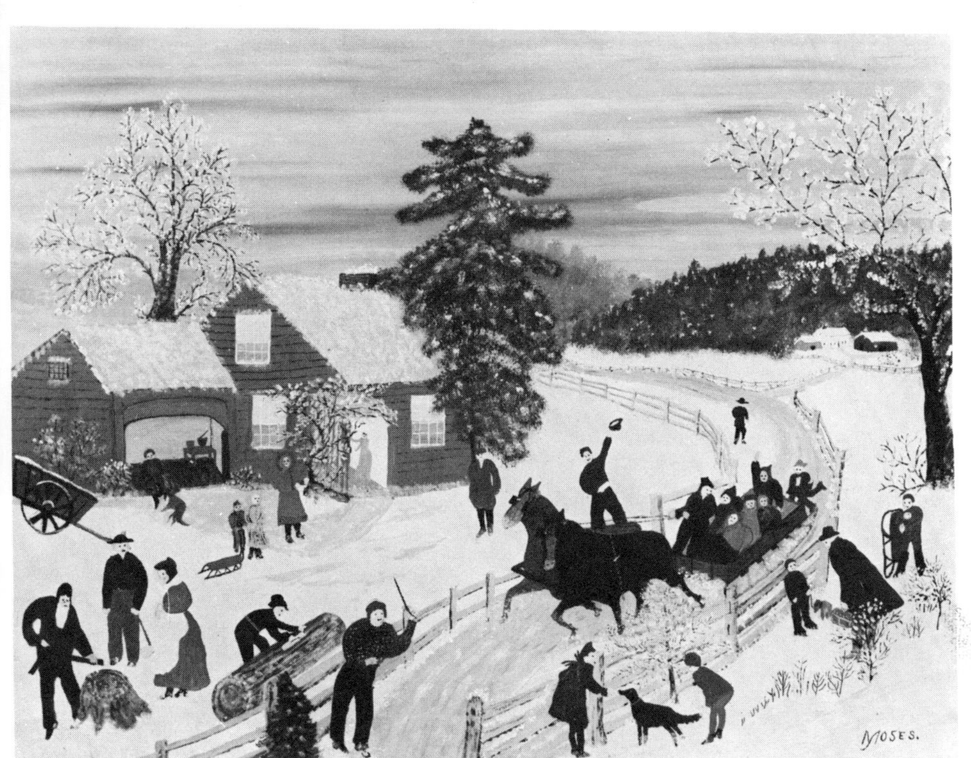

133

JOY RIDE. 1953

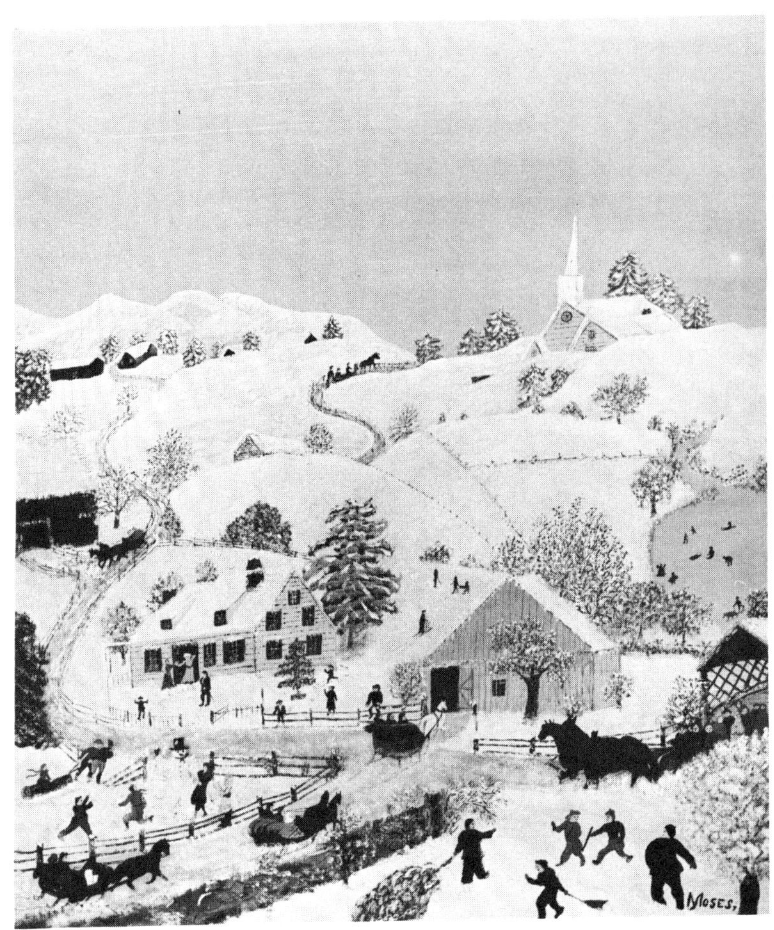

134

WHITE CHRISTMAS. 1954

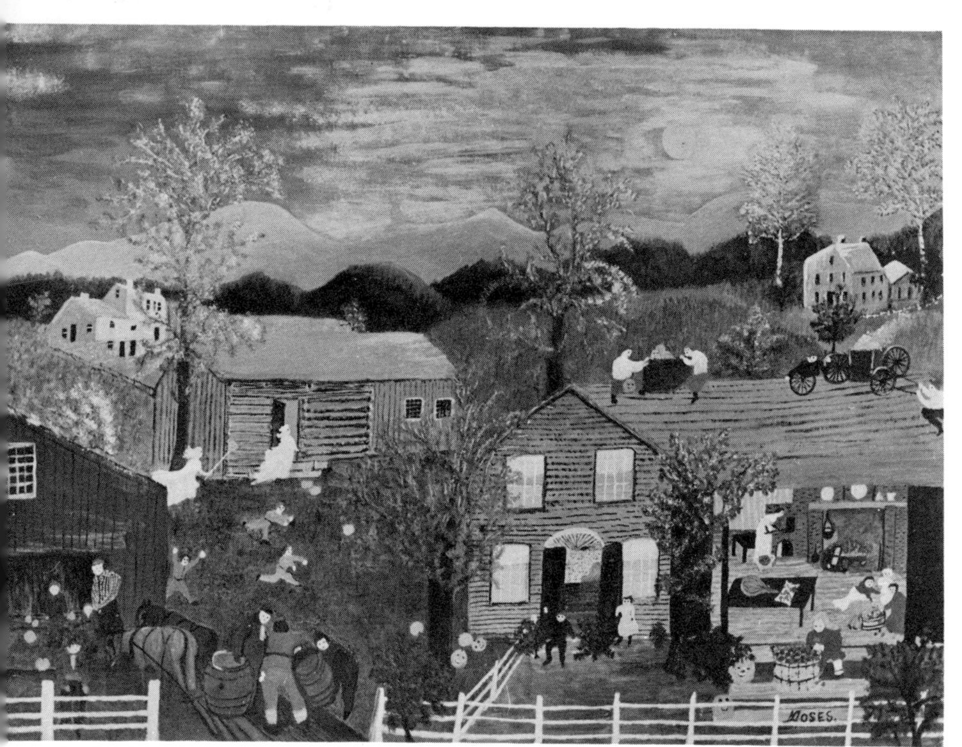

35

HALLOWEEN. 1955

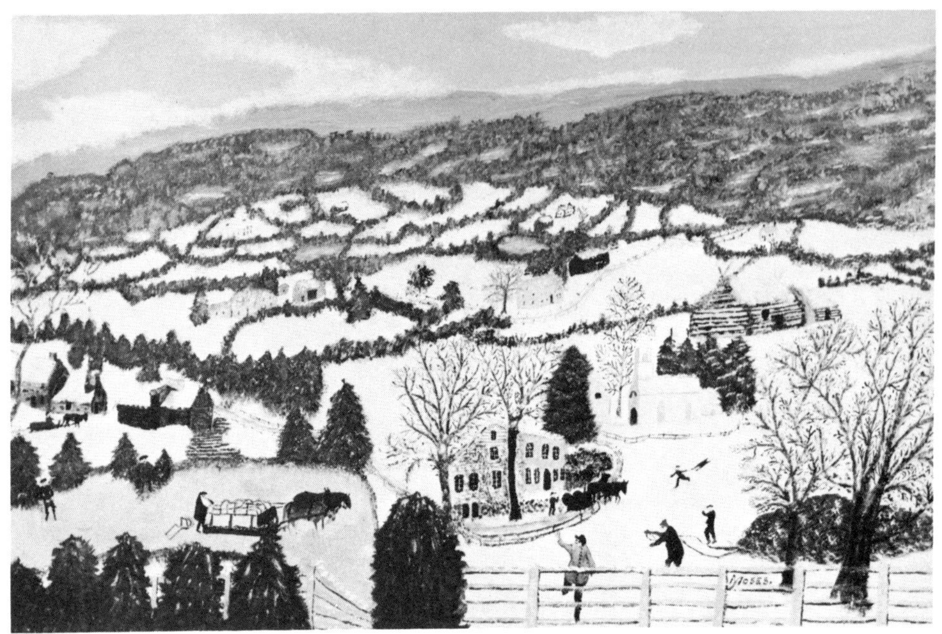

136

HELP. 1956

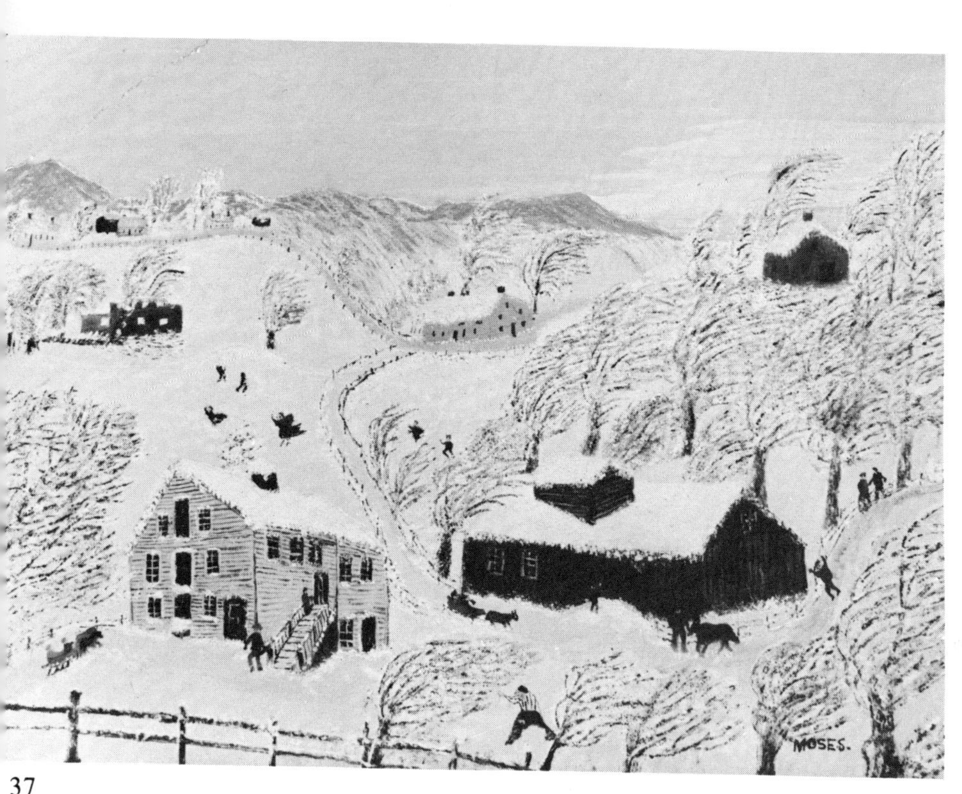

37

SNOWED IN. 1957

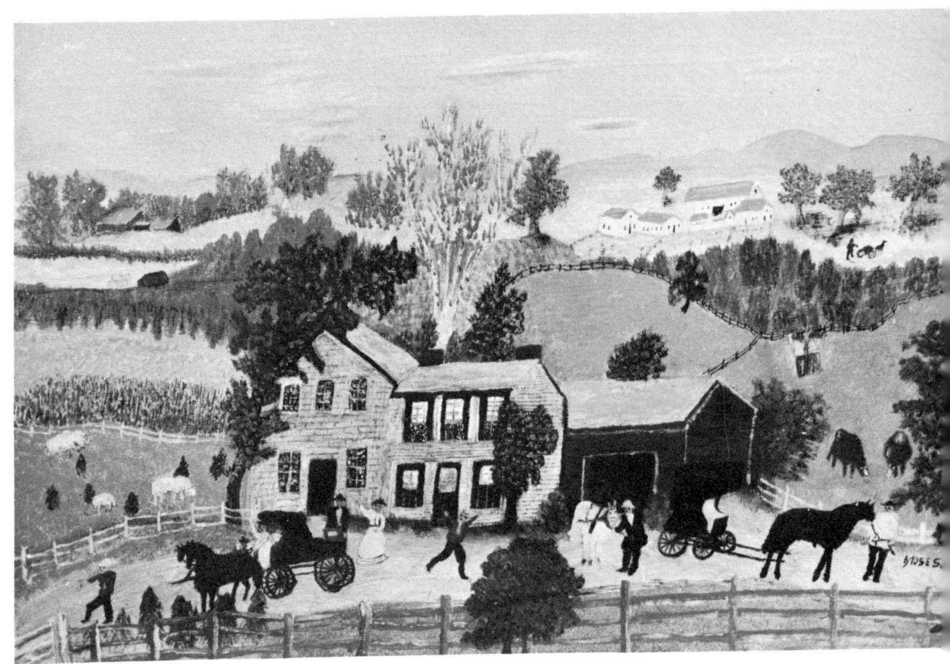

144

NOON TIME. 1959

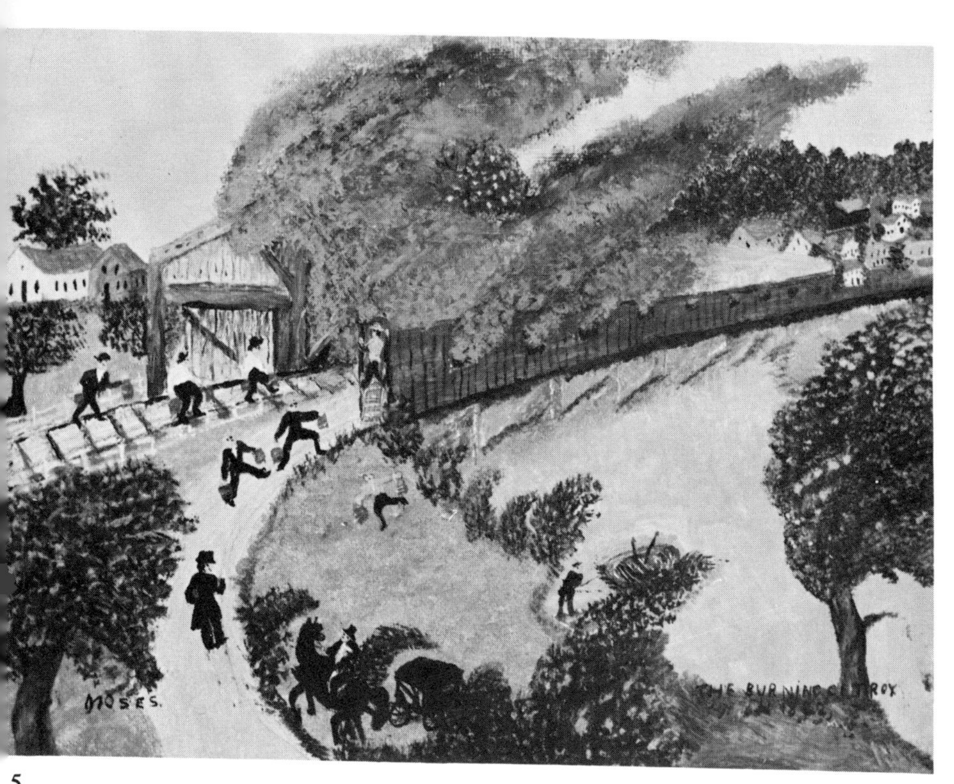

5

GREAT FIRE. 1959

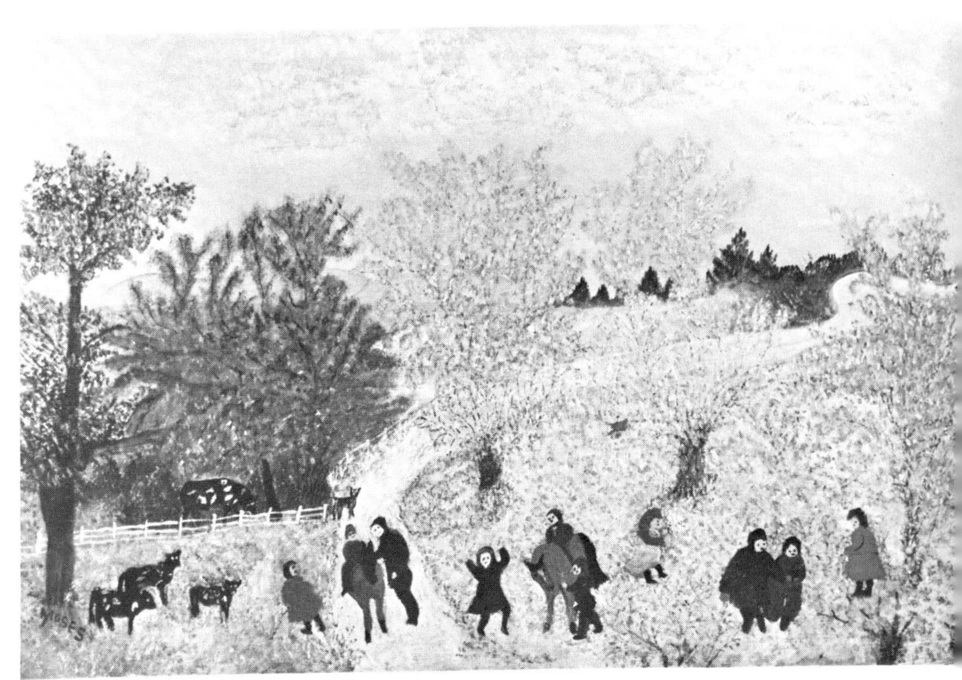

146

AUTUMN LEAVES. 1959

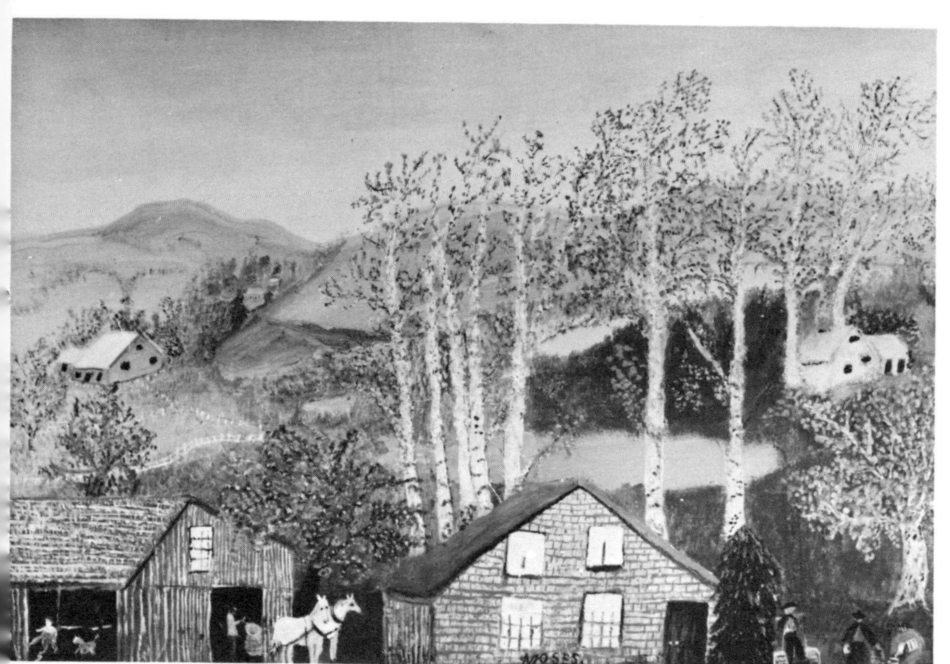

148

WHITE BIRCHES. 1961

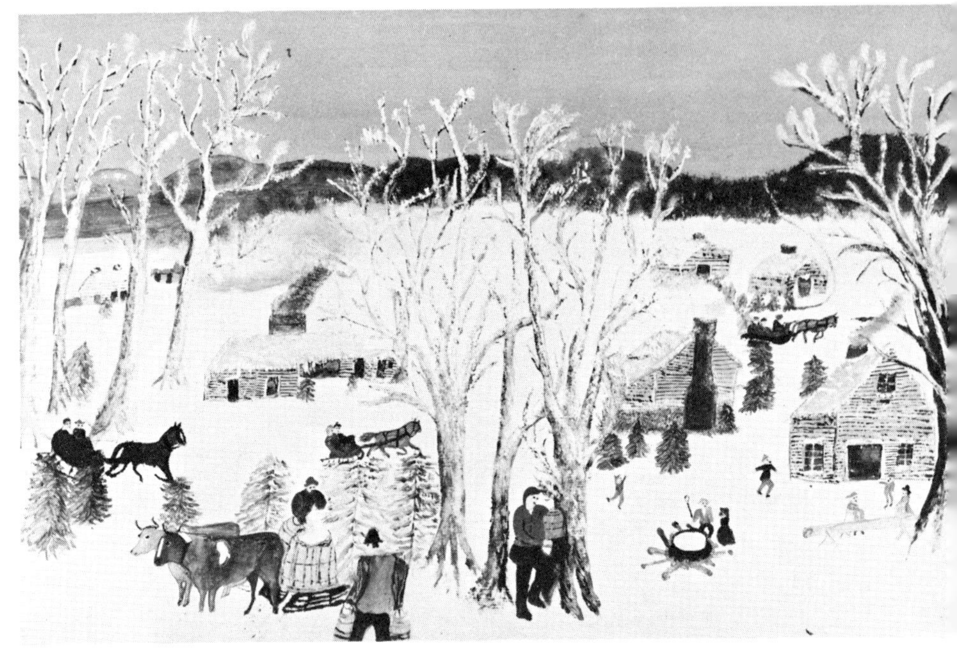

147

SUGARING OFF (unfinished). 1960